MW00451835

Web Publishing

with **N E T S C A P E**

FOR BUSY PEOPLE

Web Publishing

with **N E T S C A P E**

FOR BUSY PEOPLE

Christian Crumlish
and
Malcolm Humes

Osborne/**McGraw-Hill**

Berkeley / New York / St. Louis / San Francisco / Auckland / Bogotá

Hamburg / London / Madrid / Mexico City / Milan / Montreal / New Delhi

Panama City / Paris / São Paulo / Singapore / Sydney / Tokyo / Toronto

Osborne/**McGraw-Hill**
2600 Tenth Street
Berkeley, California 94710
U.S.A.

For information on translations or book distributors outside the U.S.A., or to arrange bulk purchase discounts for sales promotions, premiums, or fundraisers, please contact Osborne/**McGraw-Hill** at the above address.

Web Publishing with Netscape for Busy People

1234567890 DOC 99876

ISBN 0-07-882144-4

Publisher: Brandon A. Nordin
Acquisitions Editor: Joanne Cuthbertson
Project Editor: Claire Splan
Copy Editor: Timothy Barr
Proofreader: Sally Engelfried
Indexer: Valerie Robbins
Graphic Artists: Richard Whitaker, Lance Ravella
Computer Designers: Roberta Steele, Leslee Bassin, Peter F. Hancik
Quality Control: Joe Scuderi
Series and Cover Designer: Ted Mader Associates
Series Illustrator: Daniel Barbeau

to our mothers

Gabrielle Crumlish
and
Elizabeth Dill Hume

About the Authors

Christian Crumlish, publisher of the multimedia Web magazine *Enterzone*, is a writer of computer books, stories, and hyperfiction. He is the author of *The Internet for Busy People*, *Word for Windows 95 for Busy People,* and *The Internet Dictionary*.

Web maestro Malcolm Humes has been creating cutting-edge World Wide Web documents since before Netscape was invented. He has worked as the Webmaster of the City of Berkeley and is a well-recognized expert on dynamic and animated Web pages. He's currently working behind the scenes at Total Entertainment Network, bringing interactive multiplayer games to the Internet.

Contents at a glance

Contents

ACKNOWLEDGMENTS

The computer world evolves swiftly enough as it is, but the growth of the Internet—and the World Wide Web in particular—is ridiculous! We felt the ground moving underneath our feet a few times on this project, and we'd like to thank everyone we worked with for being so flexible and for coping so well with the long development time on this book.

Thanks to Joanne Cuthbertson for holding our feet to the fire and our noses to the grindstone. Ted Mader's witty, sophisticated design, built around Dan Barbeau's frazzled, contemporary people-oids, set the tone for the project and kept our minds firmly focused on you, the kind of person who needs a book like this.

Our copyeditor, Timothy Barr, helped weave together our writing styles and make it all sound fluid and sensible. Project Editor Claire Splan stuck with us through thick and thin, holding the book together.

Technical Editor Thomas Powell provided helpful and patient second-guessing, and prevented us from committing several howlers! It was a pleasure to work with someone as well versed in the subject as he.

The art and production team, headed by Roberta Steele and including Leslee Basin, Jani Beckwith, Richard Whitaker, Lance Ravella, and Peter F. Hancik, produced beautiful galleys that required a minimum of correction and polishing before they turned into final pages.

Thanks to the pioneers of Web design in the early '90s whose pages we studied carefully back when we were getting started. Thanks also the Antiweb gang who frequently offered suggestions, advice, guru insights, and humor. A nicer and more irreverent group of web designers, writers, and artists you'll never meet. Thanks especially to Janan Platt who read the entire manuscript voluntarily.

INTRODUCTION

With the Internet and the rest of the computer world changing so rapidly, it's almost impossible to keep up, even if you work in this field! On top of that, with the overall "downsizing" crunch that's been rippling through the world economy, most of us are doing what used to be considered two or three different jobs, all at once. Who can blame you if you haven't mastered the latest version of Microsoft this or Netscape that? We've written this book with busy people in mind—people who know how to operate their computers but don't have the time or energy to research and compare all the various sources of information on the latest thing.

Instead, we've filtered and boiled down our expertise and experience to serve you up a concentrated and to-the-point briefing on just exactly what you need to know about publishing on the Web *and nothing more*. There are myriad ways to create Web documents and weave together Web sites, so we've chosen an approach that is available to everyone and that takes most of the arcane details out of your hands: using Netscape Navigator Gold and its Netscape Editor module. We think that a busy person with plenty else to do besides type a lot of HTML code will appreciate a handy tool that requires little more than knowing how to work a Web browser and how to use a generic word processing program.

WE KNOW YOU'RE IN A HURRY

Let's agree to dispense with the traditional computer book preliminaries. You've probably used a mouse, held down two keys at once, and have heard of this vast global network called the Internet.

Ideally, you've browsed around the Web a little yourself. (You wouldn't try writing a book if you'd never read one, would you?)

The first chapter will introduce you to Netscape Navigator Gold and the benefits of just hanging around within the Netscape window for all your Web browsing *and* publishing needs. Chapter 2 will help you plan your site and think through what you're trying to achieve and how to accomplish it. Chapter 3 will tell you just enough about HTML to understand what's possible and what ain't.

If you'd like to forgo all preliminaries and start cranking out pages, jump directly to Chapter 4, which tells you how to get your documents started. The next few chapters cover the basics of Web-page development, including formatting text and making lists, inserting the hyperlinks that connect everything together, and adding illustrations to keep your pages from being dry as dust.

When you're ready to increase the sophistication of your pages and site design, the next three chapters will take you through incorporating multimedia objects into your pages, using tables to create great-looking page layouts, and putting in HTML codes by hand to achieve effects that aren't yet built into Netscape Editor. Chapter 12 will give you a start on some of the more advanced Web tricks, such as image maps, forms, and dynamic scripts.

When your site is ready for prime time, the final chapter will tell you how and where to publish it so people all over the globe can find your site and drop by. We won't neglect the crucial steps that come after publishing pages as well: promoting the site and keeping it up to date.

Accessing the Internet with Windows or Other Computers

This book uses examples and illustrations showing the Windows 95 versions of Netscape and other programs and features, but all of the information in the book applies equally well to other types of computers and operating systems, including earlier versions of Windows, Macintosh, and UNIX systems.

Things You Might Want to Know About This Book

You can read this book more or less in any order. We suggest cruising Chapter 1 and reading Chapter 2 first, but you can start just as easily with Chapter 4 or by jumping ahead to whatever topics are new or interesting for you. Use the book as a reference. When you're stuck, not sure how to do something, know there's an answer but not what it is, pick up the book, zero in on the answer to your question, and put the book down again. Besides clear, coherent explanations of the ins and outs of Web publishing, you'll also find some special elements to help you get the most out of Netscape. Here's a quick run down of the other elements in this book.

Fast Forward

Each chapter begins with a section called Fast Forward. They should always be your first stop if you are a confident user, or impatient or habitually late. You might find everything you need to get back in stride. Think of them as the *Reader's Digest* version of each chapter. This shorthand may leave you hungry, especially if you are new to the Internet. So, for more complete and leisurely explanations of techniques and shortcuts, read the rest of the chapter.

The Fast Forward sections are, all together, a book within a book, a built-in quick reference guide, summarizing the key tasks explained in each chapter. If you're a fast learner, or somewhat experienced, this may be the only material you need. Written step-by-step, point-by-point, they also contain page references to guide you to the more complete information later in the chapter.

Habits & Strategies

Habits & Strategies suggest time-saving tips, techniques, and worthwhile addictions. (Look for the man at the chessboard.) Force yourself to develop some good habits now, when it's still possible! These sidebars also give you the big picture and help you plan ahead.

Bookmarks

Bookmarks are easy-to-find listings of Web addresses sprinkled throughout the book. Any time you start wondering "Where did I see that link?" or "What was the reference again?" just flip open the book and scan for bookmarks and you'll find the Web site you were looking for in no time. Better yet, while reading the book, why not just go ahead and make your *own* bookmarks in Netscape whenever you see one on the page.

World Wide Web addresses, also called URLs, are notoriously long and strangely punctuated. Often, a Web address will not fit on a single line of text. To avoid introducing spurious characters that will make the addresses actually incorrect, Web addresses are wrapped without hyphens or any other special characters added, usually after a slash (/) or dot (.) character. So, for example, to visit **http://ezone.org/ez/e7/articles/xian/spam.html**, just type the entire address on one line without any spaces or breaks (and don't type the comma at the end—that's just part of this sentence).

Cautions

Sometimes it's too easy to plunge ahead and fall down a rabbit hole, resulting in hours of extra work just to get you back to where you were before you went astray. This hard hat will warn you before you commit time-consuming mistakes.

Definitions

Usually, we explain computer or networking jargon in the text, wherever the technobabble first occurs. But if you encounter words you don't recognize, look for this body builder in the margin. Definitions point out important terms you might not know the meaning of. When necessary, they're strict and a little technical, but most of the time they're informal and conversational.

Trends

We can't overemphasize how fast the Web is evolving. We're filling you in on the state-of-the-art today, but we also want to give you a heads up on what's coming down the pike in the near future. Most chapters have one or two Trends sidebars that will fill you in on where the Web is going and what to look out for.

Let's Do It!

Ready? Lets dive into Web Publishing before the next big thing comes along! Incidentally, we're happy to hear your reactions, feedback, or even corrections to this book. You can reach us through the publisher or on the Net (**xian@pobox.com** and **mal@emf.net**).

CHAPTER 1

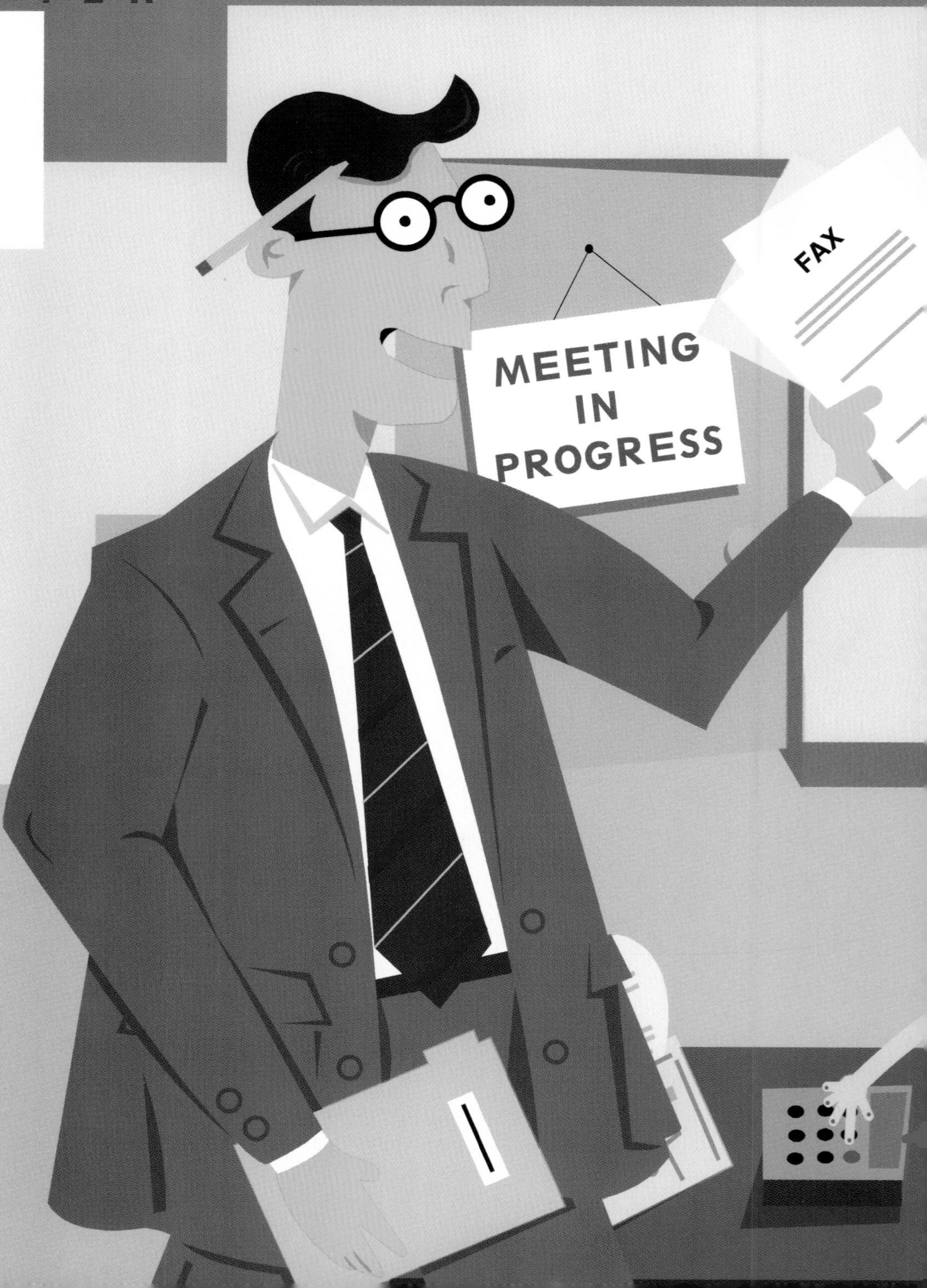

Welcome to the Netscape "Environment"

1

Netscape Navigator

FAST FORWARD

BROWSE THE WEB WITH NETSCAPE NAVIGATOR ➤ *pp. 4-6*

Start the program and *then*

- Start clicking links
- Type an address in the Location box *or*
- Choose a bookmark

News Server	☑ Unread
⊟ 🗐 news.pbinet.com (default news host)	
🗐 **news.announce.newusers**	☑ 17
🗐 **news.newusers.questions**	☑ 4415
🗐 **news.answers**	☑ 1160
🗐 **rec.music.gdead**	☑ 1038

READ NEWS OR MAIL WITH NAVIGATOR ➤ *pp. 6-8*

1. Select Window|Netscape Mail or Window|Netscape News.
2. If reading news, choose a newsgroup to read in the upper-left frame.
3. Choose a thread or message in the upper-right frame.
4. Read the message in the main (bottom) frame.

Whirled-Wide Med

The Anecdote to Civilization

No matter where in the world our travel agency flings you, you'll feel like you're hugging the Mediterranean Sea. Bring the Med with you wherever you whirl!

CREATE A WEB DOCUMENT ➤ *pp. 9-13*

You can either

- Type regular text and HTML tags into a text editor
- Convert an existing document into a Web document
- Use a raw-HTML editor to insert tags into a text document *or*
- Use a WYSIWYG editor such as Navigator Gold to type and format the document

Edit

EDIT AN EXISTING WEB DOCUMENT WITH NAVIGATOR GOLD ➤ *pp. 13-16*

1. Connect to the site with Navigator.
2. Click the Edit button.
3. Save the document.
4. Edit the document.
5. Click the Publish button.

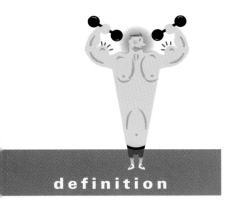

The Web: The World Wide Web, a network of linked information servers on the Internet, that can be accessed easily by lay people and can display text, pictures, and other objects.

habits & strategies

Before you even start working on your site, be sure to spend some time "surfing" the Net, visiting related (or competing) sites, and stockpiling ideas.

Just at the time the Internet was becoming an overnight sensation, when most of us were getting used to the idea of a worldwide network of linked computers and the sudden ability to send e-mail to anyone and everyone, the World Wide Web sprang onto the scene, turning up the volume even more. It seems like nearly every company, big or small, is putting itself on the Web, along with all kinds of other organizations, and, of course, individuals.

You may have heard that HTML (the language used to create documents on the Web) is actually pretty easy to learn, but you know how that really goes. No matter how easy or straightforward something on the computer purports to be, the fact of the matter is that you'll have to spend 10 or 20 hours studying the subject and going through various trial-and-error experiments until you're comfortable. We have a lot of friends who've told us they're "just about to learn HTML," and are planning to make a Web site real soon. Up till now, the only people who've actually done it were those willing to slog through the busy-work involved in making and fixing HTML documents.

Fortunately, the task really has just gotten a lot easier. That's because the tools that help people create Web documents (that is to say, tools for regular people, not for programmers!) keep maturing, getting better and more sophisticated, and there's a furious competition out there among these products to win the "mindshare" of the next generation of Internet-savvy people. No matter how busy you are, you can now use a Web-editing program such as Navigator Gold's Netscape Editor to start putting together a home page or even a full-fledged Web site.

As we just mentioned, there are many Web-creation tools out there on the market. We believe that the tool to choose if you're too busy to learn HTML is Netscape Navigator Gold. In the rest of this chapter, we'll give you a sense of how the Web has gotten to the state it's in now, and why Netscape's solution is the right one for busy people. If you feel like you can safely dispense with the background, then jump

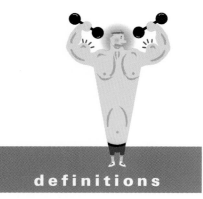

definitions

Web page: *Any hypertext document on the Web.*

hypertext: *Text that contains links to other text.*

home page: *An individual's personal Web page; the Web page a browser starts on; the first or main page of a Web site.*

Web site: *A fully developed Web presence, composed of interrelated Web pages.*

ahead to the section near the end of this chapter called "Publishing Web Documents with Netscape Navigator Gold" to find out how to download a copy of the software used in this book and get right to work.

THE NETSCAPE STRATEGY

So why Netscape? Well, over the last couple of years, Netscape has been shaping its product into the most useful, full-featured Internet program available, making it nearly indispensable. Netscape very cleverly gave away the first version of its browser for free, establishing a very wide installed base. Some estimates suggest that nearly three-quarters of all people browsing the Web are doing so with some version of Netscape Navigator. With such a large piece of the Web audience seeing things through the Netscape lens, it makes a lot of sense to develop Web sites using the Netscape platform.

Christian's Mini-History of the Web

So what can Navigator do? Christian's experience with the Web will help illustrate this, so he'll take over for now and send Malcolm off to do some crystal ball-gazing and to set up some of the advanced examples (such as frames) near the end of the book.

State-of-the-Art Web Browser

There may be a few other Web browsers that are comparable to Navigator (Microsoft's Internet Explorer is nearly giving it a run for its money, at least on the Windows platform), but there's no denying the Navigator is the cream of the crop. When I first got on the Internet, it was generally accepted that users would have to gain some basic familiarity with UNIX and master a selection of separate tools (a mail program, a news reader, a Telnet program, a Gopher client, and others) for performing the various actions and tasks online. The first Web browser I ever saw was Lynx, a character-only browser that runs in a Unix shell environment (see Figure 1.1).

I started hearing rumors about a graphical Web browser called Mosaic, designed by people at NCSA (the National Center for Supercomputer Applications) at the University of Illinois, but I had to get myself a direct-access dial-up account before I could run that sort of browser. As soon as I got a chance to really use Mosaic, I realized that

```
Netcom - HyperTerminal                                    _ 5 X
File  Edit  View  Call  Transfer  Help

 D 🖙  🕾 ⅗  🗔 🖻  🖆

                              The Busy Person's Links (pl of 10)
                         THE BUSY PERSON'S LINKS

            Email  Christian if a link is out-of-date or broken.

            Web | Mail & Lists | Usenet & Newsreaders | IRC (Chat) | FTP, Telnet, &
            Gopher
            Directories | Searching | Places to Start | Web Publishing | Setting Up

      The World Wide Web

                 * WWW FAQ
                 * W3 Consortium (Who "runs" the Web?)
                 * Netscape Navigator
                 * Internet Explorer
                 * Yahoo (a directory of the Web)
                 * Enterzone (a Web 'zine)
                 * Project Gutenberg (a gopher site)
                 * news.announce.newusers (a newsgroup)
                 * mal's web of vicarious delusions
      -- press space for more, use arrow keys to move, '?' for help, 'q' to quit
         Arrow keys: Up and Down to move. Right to follow a link; Left to go back.
         H)elp O)ptions P)rint G)o M)ain screen Q)uit /=search [delete]=history list
```

Figure 1.1 Although it's not a point-and-click browser and it can't display images, Lynx is still a very fast and easy way to navigate the Web (and hence, the Internet).

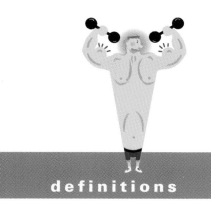

definitions

Gopher: *A method of making Internet resources available in the form of menus or folders.*

FTP: *File Transfer Protocol, the standard way of moving files around the Net.*

it was what we call in the computer industry a "killer app," a program so compelling that it would sell large numbers of people on the efficacy of a new technology. Suddenly, sifting through the Internet and finding information and programs became as easy as pointing and clicking.

I also realized that the Web was the perfect way to distribute (or, should I say, publish) information on the Internet, and I started working on a free online magazine called *Enterzone* (see Figure 1.2).

Part of the beauty of Web browsers is that, in addition to providing easy access to the Web, they also eliminate the need for at least part of the set of Internet tools the old-time user had to accumulate. The Web ate Gopher, for one thing. There's nothing you can do with a Gopher client program that you can't do with a Web browser. Most of the uses for FTP (copying files from remote archive sites, for example), are also more easily achieved with a Web browser.

To make a long story short, much of the team of programmers that developed NCSA Mosaic moved to California to work for a new start-up company that, at the time, was calling itself Mosaic Communications Corp. They put together a new Web browser—at first called

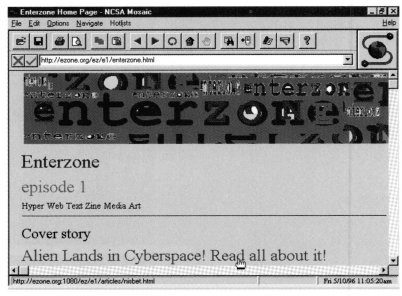

Figure 1.2 Here's how the first "episode" of *Enterzone* looks on the current version of Mosaic.

Mosaic Netscape, then just Netscape, and now Netscape Navigator—that was the equal of any other browser out there, at least as good as NCSA Mosaic, and (at the time) equally free.

Netscape Navigator has turned out to be the most popular Web browser of them all. Besides offering the hyperlinking every browser makes available and the graphics that have been standard since Mosaic, Navigator includes functional improvements, such as the ability to click a link on a page that has not yet fully loaded, and cutting-edge features, such as the ability to accommodate "plug-in" programs to incorporate sophisticated multimedia content into Web presentations.

But there are other features of the Internet besides the World Wide Web that most users want to take advantage of, and successive releases of Navigator have added capabilities for dealing with each of these, as the next few sections will explain.

More-than-Adequate News Reader

As I alluded to, all Web browsers can perform some of the functions of other, predecessor Internet tools. Mosaic and Netscape

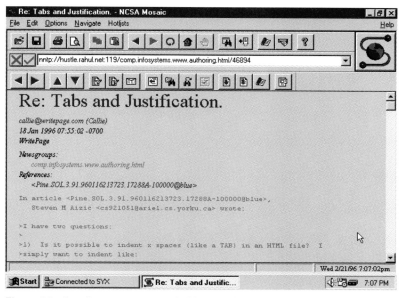

Figure 1.3 Reading a newsgroup in Mosaic. Those funky colors are not customizable.

Navigator versions 1.*x* had a fairly simple way of displaying news articles, with the added advantage that any Web addresses mentioned in newsgroup posts appear as clickable hyperlinks (see Figure 1.3).

Since then, most pure newsreaders—as well as some mail programs—are adding this feature, enabling a mouse-click on a Web address to start up an external Web browser pointed at that address.

Full-Featured Mail Program

When Netscape first started floating its beta (almost-ready-for-prime-time) version of Navigator 2.0, they unveiled a complete mail module along with a fully redesigned news interface. It had always been possible to send a mail message from within Navigator, but until this version, Netscape could not be used as an e-mail client program—handling incoming mail, sorting mail into folders, and so on. With this added functionality, Navigator suddenly gained the ability to challenge even the most popular Internet mail clients such as Eudora and Pegasus Mail. Figure 1.4 shows Navigator's e-mail window.

CAUTION

As fast as Netscape adds features to its e-mail program, it's still behind the curve as far as dedicated mail programs go, which are adding new abilities all the time. So, Netscape is still no Eudora, for example.

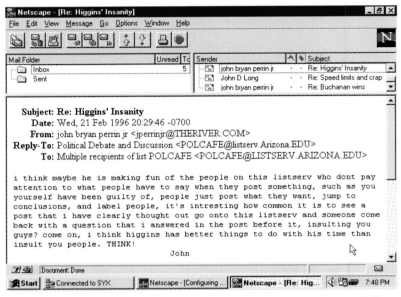

Figure 1.4 Navigator's e-mail module is now nearly as useful as most dedicated mail clients. Its redesigned news interface is nearly identical to the mail window (with frames—windowpanes—for newsgroups, subjects, and articles instead of mailboxes, subjects, and messages).

trends

Netscape's mail and news clients are not quite as good as their best, state-of-the-art, dedicated competitors (for instance: Eudora and Pegasus are better mail programs, and NewsWatcher and Agent are better newsreaders), but they are still quite credible. Their addition to the standard navigator package continues the trend of making a Web browser into an all-in-one program for just about every Internet task. The most recent versions of Navigator, for example, have almost completely co-opted stand-alone FTP programs, enabling you to upload (send) files to an FTP site by dragging their icons into the browser window.

habits & strategies

You may want to use Netscape for as many of your Internet tasks as possible, just to keep your life simple. The fewer different programs you have to download, install, and learn, the better!

CAUTION

You could easily lose hours of valuable time if you get engrossed in typing HTML tags and then tweaking them by hand to perfect your pages.

So you see, at least from the user's point of view, Netscape is positioning its Navigator product as the single, indispensable Internet tool.

HOW TO CREATE WEB DOCUMENTS

While all of this development of Internet tools has been going on, the process of creating content for the World Wide Web has been slowly getting a little easier. Depending on your goals and your background, there are still several ways to create Web documents.

Typing HTML Tags By Hand (the "Old-Fashioned" Way)

Back when I (and my cohorts) started publishing *Enterzone,* we had to create Web documents by typing all kinds of HTML tags into plain text documents. This was not impossible, but it was frustrating and tedious. Back then, most of the people creating Web sites were programmers, graduate students, researchers, and technology companies, and most of these people were willing to put up with and learn the hardcore details of HTML.

The best analogy for that approach to making Web documents would be an early word-processing program. If you remember WordStar or even the EDLIN text editor that used to come with MS-DOS, then you have some idea of how this approach to document-creation works.

In the end it was rewarding, since a fairly crude looking text document with a bunch of ugly <CODE>s embedded in it would end up looking quite snazzy indeed when viewed in a Web browser. Figure 1.5 shows part of the HTML source document underlying the home page of the first *Enterzone* episode (shown in Mosaic in Figure 1.2).

To be totally honest, I still code a lot of HTML documents myself this way, though I wouldn't wish it on anyone who doesn't harbor a little bit of geekery in their soul. I do it now only because I've already put the time in to learn the tags and I often consider it faster to simply type them in myself than to format a document using some other tool. Not

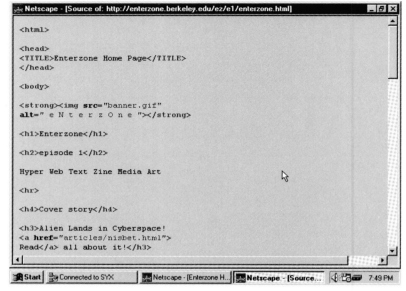

```
Netscape - [Source of: http://enterzone.berkeley.edu/ez/e1/enterzone.html]

<html>

<head>
<TITLE>Enterzone Home Page</TITLE>
</head>

<body>

<strong><img src="banner.gif"
alt=" e N t e r z O n e "></strong>

<h1>Enterzone</h1>

<h2>episode 1</h2>

Hyper Web Text Zine Media Art

<hr>

<h4>Cover story</h4>

<h3>Alien Lands in Cyberspace!
<a href="articles/nisbet.html">
Read</a> all about it!</h3>
```

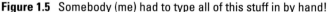

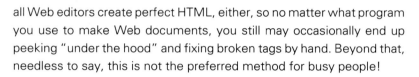

Figure 1.5 Somebody (me) had to type all of this stuff in by hand!

all Web editors create perfect HTML, either, so no matter what program you use to make Web documents, you still may occasionally end up peeking "under the hood" and fixing broken tags by hand. Beyond that, needless to say, this is not the preferred method for busy people!

Tag-Insertion Shortcuts and Converters

Clearly there was a need for shortcuts! Even the most techie-oriented type hates repetition and gets bored of typing. Since the basic set of HTML tags doesn't change from document to document, people started developing macros (recorded shortcuts) for word processing programs and even stand-alone HTML-tag editor tools. Some of these tools featured specialized aids for Web document creation, such as the ability to remember all the Web addresses inserted into a document (so that any one of them could be chosen from a list when needed again in the future).

There are too many such tools out there now for me to mention them all, and they range from add-ins to word processors, to one-purpose converter programs, to stand-alone HTML editors (some of which are quite buggy still). One very popular converter is called rtf2html. It converts documents from RTF (rich text format) to HTML, as the name implies. RTF encodes some of the most common formatting features (such as boldface and italics) using regular text characters.

bookmark

*You can download rtf2html from **ftp://oac.hsc.uth.tmc.edu/public/ unix/WWW/** or see the Web Designer HTML Converters and Templates page at **http://www.kosone.com:81/nelsonl/convert.htm** for other options.*

These days, it seems that HotDog is the most popular HTML editor for the PC, and BB Edit (a shareware editor with HTML extensions) is a popular favorite for the Mac.

Converters (either a program designed for that single task or an editor that has that capability) make it feasible for people without the time to study, practice, and master HTML to make Web documents. They also ease the development of Web sites by making it easier to adapt existing documents to the Web format.

These HTML editors were definitely a step up from using plain text editors and typing in all the tags by hand. For the technically inclined, they're the perfect compromise, providing shortcuts for repetitive tasks but still showing the embedded HTML tags.

If you've ever worked with WordPerfect for DOS, which kept documents in a clean, text-oriented style and enabled users to reveal hidden formatting codes whenever needed, then you have some idea of what it's like to work with an HTML editor.

What You See is What You Get (More or Less)

Ultimately, the compelling solution for most people is one that does not require that you learn any more skills but instead draws on your familiar experiences. Thus, WYSIWYG Web editors started coming down the pike. WYSIWYG (What You See is What You Get) means that

habits & strategies

If you want to adapt your existing documents for your Web site, and a lot are already in Word format, then you'll definitely want to download Internet Assistant from the Microsoft Web site (http://www.microsoft.com) and use it to convert those documents.

the editor attempts to display for you the intended result—the way the document will appear when opened in a Web browser—instead of the underlying HTML tags. This is closer to the more familiar word processing model as exemplified by Word for Windows or just about any word processor on the Macintosh. While working on your document, you see something as close as possible to the final result (printed, in the case of word processors). If you change normal text into a heading, its appearance changes.

The most popular WYSIWYG Web editor up to now has been PageMill, which was developed for the Macintosh but has recently been released as a Windows version.

PageMill isn't perfect: BB Edit has actually added a feature to "clean up" the incorrect HTML coding the PageMill can sometimes create in a document. But it's very intuitive to use, allowing you to simply point and click on graphics or links and to put them in place and format them. Around the time I started working on this book, Microsoft bought Vermeer, the maker of an up-and-coming Web editor called Front Page. Other entries in this category include NaviSoft and, to some extent, Microsoft's Internet Assistant.

bookmark

*Microsoft is at **http://www.microsoft.com**.*

Microsoft's Internet Assistant add-in for Word for Windows (and WordPerfect's equivalent Internet Publisher add-in) makes the most popular word processing program into a pretty decent Web editor and, with its ability to save existing Word documents in an HTML format, a fine converter to boot.

As products like these compete to offer the most full-fledged Web creation solution, they've started adding tools to assist in the creation of some of the trickier elements of Web documents, such as tables and clickable image maps. Even a hard-core, old-fashioned HTML jockey such as myself gets frustrated when trying to assemble the correct tags

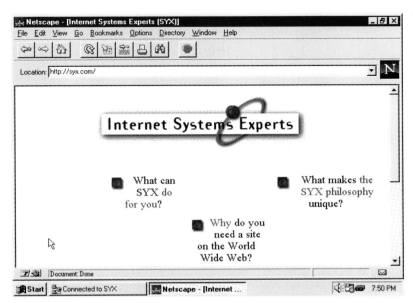

Figure 1.6 The Internet Systems Experts (SYX) home page includes a tricky table with blank cells in order to create an asymmetrical layout. No way did I want to type the tags in for that table by hand!

for a complicated table, such as the one used for my company's home page (see Figure 1.6).

Navigator Gold to the Rescue

Into this fray has come Netscape's latest extension of the Navigator tool, Netscape Navigator Gold 3.0. In typical Netscape fashion, it codifies the process of making an HTML document quite nicely, without quite matching the top-of-the-line WYSIWYG editor tools feature-for-feature (yet), and it has the added convenience of being seamlessly integrated into the popular Web-browser interface we've all come to know and love. Finally, you can start creating content for the Web with the ease you've come to expect for making documents on your own computer. Point Navigator at the page you want to work on, save the current version to your disk, go into edit mode, change the document,

and then post it back to the Web site with the press of a single button. What could be simpler? Notice a typo in your home page? Just fix it.

Navigator Gold's secret weapon is Netscape Editor, which, just like the Netscape Mail and Netscape News modules, spins off its own window whenever you want to use it. The Netscape Editor window is almost identical to the familiar browser window, but (naturally) offers editing commands on menus and button bars, instead of the usual navigation commands. You can switch back and forth between the browser and the editor with the press of a button.

PUBLISHING WEB DOCUMENTS WITH NAVIGATOR GOLD

Well, that should be enough background for anyone. The next step is for you to obtain a copy of Navigator Gold and start using it. To download the latest version of Navigator Gold from the Netscape Web site, point your browser at the Netscape home page and go to the Download Software Page. Choose items in the online form (see Figure 1.7), and click the button called Click to Display Download Sites.

bookmark

To download Netscape Navigator Gold, point your Web browser to
http://home.netscape.com/comprod/mirror/index.html.

This will reload the page with a list of links to download sites now attached at the bottom (scroll down to see them). Choose one to download the product. You may have to try again if it's busy (click reload, or try a different link). If it fails more than once, try again in a few minutes. If you still have trouble getting through, try to do it at some off-peak time, such as midnight. When you have successfully downloaded the file, double-click it to start the installation process. When the installation is done, Netscape will offer to connect you to its home page to complete the registration process.

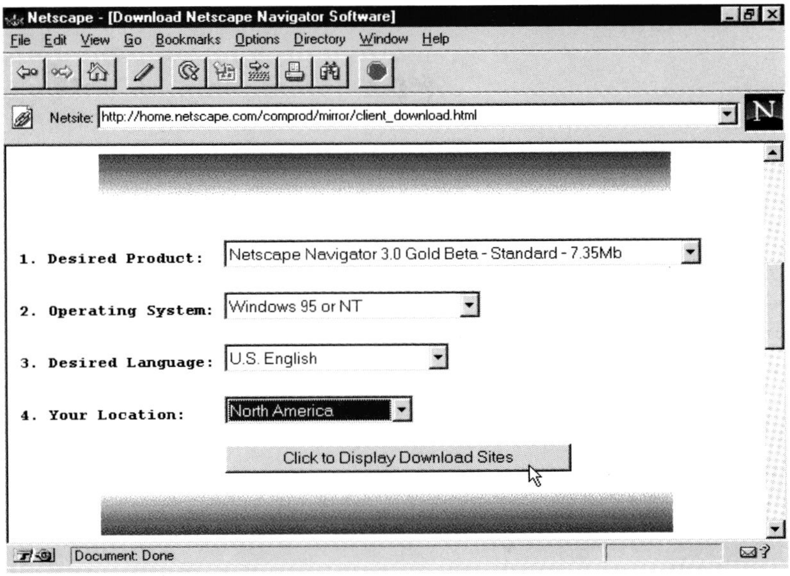

Figure 1.7 Choose Netscape Navigator Gold, your type of computer, the language you work with, and the continent you're on.

The way Netscape releases software, you can usually get a copy to evaluate for free, but if you intend to use it for business purposes, it's your legal responsibility to register and pay for the product. (If you're using the beta version of an upcoming release, you're doing them a favor and you won't have to pay for it until the product comes out for real.) The Netscape installation process always offers to connect you to the Netscape Web site when it's done installing so you can register and pay for the program if you wish.

When we started writing this book, Navigator Gold was still in its beta version 1.0, with lots of "To be done" messages on its dialog boxes and regular ugly crashes. When we had it halfway done, Netscape released the 2.0 version, which works very well, but lacked a couple of really useful tools, such as the table editor. While we're finishing up this book, Netscape is beta testing the 3.0 version (code named Atlas), which fortunately does have a table editor. A 4.0 version is expected by the end of the year, but the product is already solid.

Once you've installed Navigator Gold, you can immediately get your feet wet making Web documents by visiting the Netscape Page

Starter Site's Gold Rush Tool Chest. See Chapter 4 for more on the basic templates provided among those pages.

bookmark

The Netscape Gold Rush Tool Chest is at
http://home.netscape.com/assist/net_sites/starter/samples/index.html.

NETSCAPE AS THE INTERNET'S "PLATFORM"

Once you've got Navigator Gold ready to go, you're equipped with a single program for just about every Internet need you might have. You can stay within the Netscape "environment" all the time, sending and receiving mail, downloading and uploading files, reading and posting news, browsing the Web, and publishing Web documents. Because Netscape runs on every major computer platform, it suddenly doesn't matter all that much whether you use a Macintosh, a PC, a UNIX box, or an Eniac machine (OK, that last one's a ringer, a '50s era mega-computer with all the skills of a free calculator, circa 1980), for that matter.

As long as you're working on the Internet, Netscape can be your "platform." Sure, we realize that playing along with Netscape like this might just turn it into the next Microsoft, with a stranglehold on the entire computer-development world. But if you're a busy person, the most important thing you can have a single tool that does it all so you don't have to keep learning a new piece of software every time you want to do something different on the Net.

WHY A WEB SITE AND WHAT KIND

If you already have a very clear idea of both the sort of Web site you want to build and how you plan to organize and develop it, then you might want to skip ahead to Chapter 3 and plunge right into the process of creating HTML documents. If not, Chapter 2 should help you sort out some important issues before you get started. Decide what kind of Web site you're building, what you want it to look like, what role it should play for your users, and how you want it to behave. Think a little bit about how to organize the elements of the site, and then you'll be ready to start cranking.

Planning Your Web Site

19

FAST FORWARD

WHAT'S A WEB SITE FOR? ➤ *pp. 23-27*
A Web site is the flagship of an organization's Internet presence, the hub of an information center about the organization.

WHAT TYPE OF WEB SITE? ➤ *pp. 27-32*
Web sites can take many forms including:
- Publications
- Information kiosks
- Stores
- Support lines

DESIGNING A WEB SITE ➤ *pp. 34-37*
In planning a Web site, you have to assemble some tools (identified throughout this book) and then consider the following issues:
- What is your budget?
- What level of service can you expect to offer at your Web site?
- Who is your audience and how can you best serve them?
- What will be the content of your site?
- Will you have to develop new material?
- How will your site be designed and organized?
- What will the home page look like?
- What will the hypertext structure be?

PRODUCT	PRICE	QUANTITY	TOTAL
Netscape Commerce Server	1295.00	1	1295.00

TO THINK ABOUT AHEAD OF TIME: ➤ *pp. 37-39*

Before going "live" with a site, you'll also want to consider these issues:

- What sort of illustrations and other graphical art will you use to make your pages interesting to visit?
- To what extent will you take advantage of other media to enliven your Web site?
- Does your site need to be interactive? Will you have a form to fill out? Will the site be searchable? Will people be able to leave messages or chat live at your site?
- Will you need to be able to make sales or perform commercial transactions through your Web site?

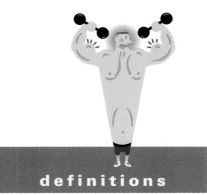

definitions

The Internet: Also "the Net," the global network of networks that enables computers everywhere to communicate with each other, transferring messages and files.
Web browser: A program (such as Netscape Navigator or the various versions of Mosaic) used to connect a user to Web sites and other Internet facilities.

The World Wide Web is also sometimes referred to as WWW, W3, w^3, and so on, but we just call it the Web throughout this book.

Just last year it was enough to have an e-mail address on your business card to show that you and your company were technologically up to date and on the Internet. Now you need an address on the World Wide Web as well. Being connected to the Net is one thing, but then there's the question of your "presence." Your Internet presence is how you appear to others on the Net, and a Web site is the central "headquarters" of that presence. One institution's presence might be akin to a P.O. Box—a blind e-mail drop with no interaction, no guaranteed response. At the other end of the spectrum, there are companies coming online whose entire business model is acted out through their interactive World Wide Web presence.

But you don't have time to learn all about the Internet and the Web, do you? You're too busy. We all are. Still, you can't afford to ignore this new arena. You wouldn't skip learning how to use a phone because you didn't have the time, would you? Fortunately, we can take you through the heart of what you need to know in this book in a few evenings or lunch breaks.

At whatever scale, the Web is a relatively cheap way to publicize and disseminate information globally, saving on the costs of paper and distribution. The Web can be a great equalizer of large and small entities. A Web site could be one lonely person in a back room or a building full of technicians. Location is relative. All the "real estate" costs about the same on the Web. (That is, every Web site is equally accessible, big or small.) Sure, huge investments of cash into design, writing, and interactivity will pay off for any site, but it's a much more level playing field than you'll find anywhere in the real world.

No matter how big or small, glamorous or bare-bones your site, you'll still have to answer the following questions: How do you get people to come and visit? How do you convince them to stay? How do you make them want to come back?

Most importantly, what do you use this new soapbox for? What information do you put out? How do you invest your Net presence with the personality of your company or organization? How often do you change or update? How interactive will your site be? How much work can you devote to the project? These are all things you have to think about before plunging into designing a Web presence.

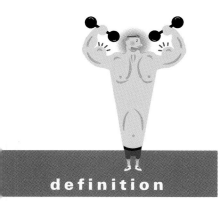

bookmark

*For more information about the Web itself, check out the WWW FAQ, which you can find on the Web, naturally, at **http://www.boutell.com/faq/** and also at the site of the World Wide Web Consortium (**http://www.w3.org**).*

definition

link: *A "live" connection to another document, object, or section of the current document, embedded in a Web page.*

HOME PAGE OR WEB SITE?

The terms "home page" and "Web site" are used somewhat interchangeably, but they are beginning to have different connotations. Home page now suggests a personal page, not unlike a biographical listing or yearbook entry. The term is also used to refer to the main page of a larger site, meaning something like home base, a page you can return to from anywhere at the site. The term Web site suggests a fully fleshed-out complex of Web pages, adding up to a coherent entity.

For a credible presence, start thinking in terms of a Web site. Technically, a site is any location on the Internet, any address. Conceptually, though, it's the place representing your organization, the sum of the substance available via the Web.

Uses for a Web Site

Before you can start planning a site, you have to think through what it will be used for. What is its purpose? This depends partly on what type of organization (or project) you're putting on the Web, whether it be a company, academic department, non-profit entity, publication, individual, or something else entirely. Here are some ideas of how you can use a Web site for the benefit of a number of different types of organizations.

Uses of a Web Site for a Company

The main uses of a Web site by a company are as an outlet for public relations, as support for marketing campaign, and as the equivalent of advertising—though it should be noted that the nature of the Internet-as-a-medium is different enough from television (because it's interactive) and print (because it's ever-changing) that a working advertising model for the Internet would naturally be something quite different from traditional ads.

For many types of companies, the Web (and judicious linking to other parts of the Internet) can help provide support to customers, possibly cheaper than phone support (and also more accessible for some, with no waiting). With trustworthy security methods in place, you can even sell your wares on the Net, making every user's Web browser into a point-of-sale machine for your business. A Web site can also serve as a personnel resource, a place to make job announcements and to screen applicants.

Most businesses benefit from good old-fashioned networking—getting together with people in related fields and with the same interests and making contacts. The Net is perfect for that, and Web sites typically contain links to other "allied" entities. Trade links with those in your electronic community. If you can attract participants, online forms make surveys easy to conduct.

Of course, different types of businesses have different goals and can make different uses of the Web. Manufacturing companies can't deliver their wares over the wires, but they can make sales and distribute information that way. Retail stores can have the equivalent of print catalogs online as well as the ability to field questions. Media companies should be able to use the Net as a medium to complement their print and broadcasting projects. Non-profit organizations and political and social movements can use the Web as an organizing tool, to connect people separated by distance, and to distribute information and plan actions cheaply.

A Web Site for an Academic Entity

An academic organization, such as a school, department, or research group, can use a Web site to make papers available, online or in downloadable formats, and to publicize course information. It can make use of online forms for applications and requests for publications. A site can offer information on faculty, courses, and projects. It can demonstrate models and data.

A Web site can include an online journal (also called e-journals) or can make useful tools available for download. An academic site could have links to related projects and admissions information. Figure 2.1 shows NSSDC's OMNIWeb site, from which the National Space Science Data Center's solar wind data can be downloaded and plotted.

Figure 2.1 National Space Science Data Center's resource for solar wind magnetic field and plasma data, energetic proton fluxes, and geomagnetic and solar activity indices. How did you get by this long without it?

bookmark

*NSSDC's OMNIWeb is at **http://nssdc.gsfc.nasa.gov/omniweb/ow.html**.*

The Web as a Publishing Medium

If you have information you want to disseminate to a broad audience (versus a captive or highly specialized one), or if you can't afford the costs of printing and distribution, then you should consider publishing your information on the Web. The Internet is alive with alternative publications. With Web server space easily available, artists can put together electronic gallery spaces and writers can publish their work to a worldwide audience.

bookmark

*Enterzone, a free Webzine published by one of the authors of this book, can be found at **http://ezone.org/ez**.*

The Web can also be used as an alternative venue for promoting public events or for organizing grass-roots political movements.

Web Site as Personal Project or Statement

All this talk of organizations and companies overlooks one of the more exciting aspects of the Web: the potential for individuals ("private citizens") to assemble and publish personal statements or self-motivated projects. At one end of the spectrum, you have the (somewhat hackneyed) personal home page, such as the type many undergraduates are posting these days. These are often a cross between a glorified bookmark list and a yearbook entry ("here's a picture of my cat").

But personal Web sites can be far more interesting and rich than that. There's nothing wrong with starting off with a list of (and links to) your favorite Web sites, but the Web is already overflowing with voluminous lists of sites. At least annotate your picks, write a few words about why you like this or that. At best, a personal Web site can grow to become more than a brief personal statement or résumé. One of our favorite home-pages-gone-wild is Levi Asher's Literary Kicks Web site (**http://www.charm.net/~brooklyn**), where he publishes his thoughts and insights about the Beat Generation writers, as well as other literary luminaries he admires. Like Tom Sawyer painting the fence, he just started pushing his writing and art out there and, before long, started getting a lot of e-mail from other people with similar interests. Soon afterward he had all kinds of volunteers contributing articles, checking information, doing interviews, and so on.

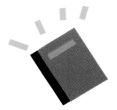

Magazine, Radio Show, Store—What's Your Metaphor?

The Web is a new medium. Like television and CD-ROMs, it is an electronic medium. Like newspapers and magazines, it's still largely a text medium (although this is changing). Like the telephone system, it is (or can be) completely two way, with every user a broadcaster.

Existing print publications, such as newspapers, are adapting their models, some more smoothly than others. *The New York Times'* first attempt at a Web presence is a "ported" version of its TimesFAX edition that requires users to download a special viewer program (called Adobe Acrobat) to start reading. Unfortunately, that extra step of obtaining helper software is a little too technical for most readers (in a year or so, though, it may not be necessary, as Web browsers expand their capabilities). Since then, the *Times* has started publishing a "proper" Web edition. To see more established Web newspapers, visit Mercury Web, SFGate, or NandO. Figure 2.2 shows an article at the NandO site.

bookmark

*The newspapers mentioned here are at **http://www.nytimes.com**, **http://www.sjmercury.com**, **http://www.sfgate.com**, and **http://www.nando.net**.*

Figure 2.2 A page from the NandO *Times,* the online newspaper of the NandO.net site.

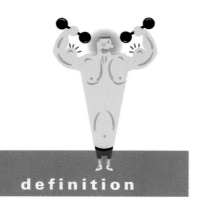

New publications have sprung up on the Web without the restrictions of coordinating with a print model. Most book publishers are using the Web to promote print releases, sometimes including short excerpts from books in their catalogs. In more bold projects, entire books have been published on the Net. Figure 2.3 shows a page from Martha Conway's serialized novel with illustrations, *In Some Unrelated Land* (Pilgrim Press, 1995).

bookmark

In Some Unrelated Land *is distributed as shareware; you can read the first half of it at **http://syx.com/pilgrim/land.html**.*

But unless you're thinking in terms of a print-style publication, these models may not work for you. The current dominant metaphor on the Web is that of the document—Web site as page or series of interrelated pages. This may change with the advent of VRML, a method

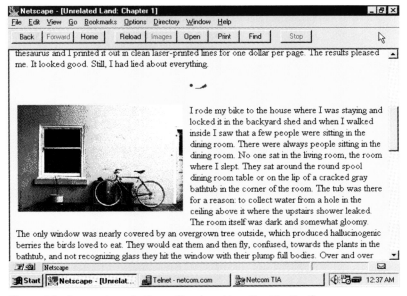

Figure 2.3 A page from *In Some Unrelated Land* by Martha Conway

of creating three-dimensional "virtual reality" spaces—Web site as place—and development tools such as Java that replace the flat, relatively non-interactive page model with the dynamic, interactive program model.

Since the medium is in its infancy, you'll most likely end up borrowing from earlier models and tweaking as necessary, but be careful not to get stuck doing things the old way when you don't need to (for instance, there's no need to schedule regular updates or releases of new information the way a periodical does—that's one possible model, but not the only one).

For instance, print publications are distributed actively (via newspaper subscription, bookstores, etc.), but the Web media are distributed passively (browsers visit your server and download files). So the Web can also be thought of as a broadcast medium. A radio show is beamed out from a transmitter and picked up by individuals within the range. Web sites are similarly broadcasting from a single point to any one who tunes in. But where radio and TV have strict schedules, Web sites are more flexible in that respect, and even audio ("radio-type") shows on the Web can be listened to at any time

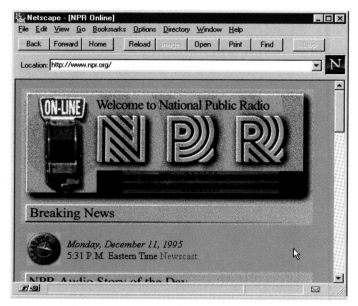

Figure 2.4 NPR puts much of its broadcasts on the Web, provides opportunities for feedback, and sells transcripts and merchandise.

(something like the video-on-demand you keep hearing about). Figure 2.4 shows how National Public Radio has addressed the question of its Web presence. When you visit that site, if your computer is equipped to play sounds, you can hear the day's regular news offerings "on demand," instead of having to tune in at a particular time as with a radio broadcast.

bookmark

*NPR's site is at **http://www.npr.org**.*

A Web site can resemble a building or storefront; the physical presence of a company. You come in the front door, take the elevator to the third floor, men's sundries, etc. The choices shown on the site's home page will help users find their way to the information they want. How do you want people to interact with your site? What do you want them to see?

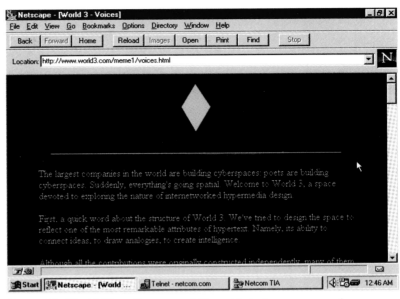

Figure 2.5 *World 3* **(http://www.world3.com)** is both gorgeous and informative

Nick Routledge's article, "Barking Up the Wrong Hierarchy," which appears in *World 3,* an e-zine for Web designers (see Figure 2.5), has some very succinct points about how a business should present itself on the Web, and I recommend reading it.

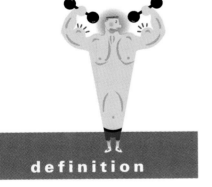

bookmark

The World 3 *site is at **http://www.world3.com**. Nick Routledge's article is at* ***http://www.world3.com/meme1/nrmark.html***.

In an important sense, your organization's Web site *is* the organization, at least in cyberspace. It's not just another publication about the organization (such as an annual report, although annual reports can of course be put on the Web), but the *place itself.* You may see some stores closing in the future to be replaced by cybershopping sites (though no doubt people will continue to want to move their bodies and see other people in the flesh when doing some of their shopping, TV's shopping channels notwithstanding).

URL, HTML, HTTP, CGI, BB King and Doris Day

Don't let the terminology scare you off. Before getting your hands dirty, brush up on the list of terms shown in Table 2.1. Don't try to understand every nuance—these terms are all technical jargon. Learn just enough to get by. Knowing what these terms mean (or being able to look them up here) should help keep you from being bewildered by consultants and experts spouting strange words and phrases.

Jargon Term	What It Means
Amber	The plug-in version of Adobe Acrobat (a program for creating portable documents).
applet	A simple program that runs when started by another program.
bandwidth	The amount of data that can flow over a connection in a set period of time. Used loosely to mean the speed of someone's connection.
CGI	Common Gateway Interface. The standard way to relate scripts and applications to Web client actions. For example, when you fill out a form at a Web page, a CGI script typically converts your input into a form the host computer can understand and produces the resulting output.
DNS	Domain Name Service. The process by which an Internet address (such as nic.cerf.net), which is relatively easy for people to deal with, is translated into a corresponding numerical address (such as 192.102.249.3).
domain	A primary organizational hierarchy of Internet addresses (such as apple.com, princeton.edu, whitehouse.gov, and so on).
host	A server or any machine to which you are connected.
HTML	Hypertext Markup Language. The code of tags used to format hypertext documents for the Web.
HTTP	Hypertext Transport Protocol. The way Web servers deliver information to Web browsers (client programs).
hypermedia	Any medium that contains links to other media (by analogy to hypertext).
hypertext	Text that contains links to other text.

Table 2.1 Some Web Terms You Should Know

Jargon Term	What It Means
image map	A graphical image that can be clicked in different areas, with different results (such as links to different page destinations) depending on where you click.
Java	A programming language used to create applets that can be sent over the Web by a server and then run on any client machine.
JavaScript	A scripting language used to stitch together traditional HTML Web documents and applets such as Java programs.
multimedia	The combination of several different media (such as text, sound, and video) into a single document or experience.
platform	A type of computer (such as a PC, a UNIX box, or a Macintosh).
protocol	An agreed-upon method of communication between two computers or pieces of software. Protocols enable computers and systems of different types to communicate.
script	A simple program, akin to a macro, consisting of a set of instructions.
server	A machine on the Internet, or a program running on it, to which other client programs can connect. A centralized repository of information or some other resource.
SGML	Standardized General Markup Language. A meta-language used to define how a specific markup language (such as HTML) will structure text.
Shockwave	The plug-in version of Macromedia Director (a program for creating multimedia presentations) for Web browsers.
site	A "place" on the Internet. The address of a server machine on the Net.
source	The written commands or code that underlie or control a Web page or applet.
streaming audio or video	The process of sending audio or video data in a continuous stream.
TCP/IP	The protocols used to send messages, files, and commands over the Internet.
URL	Uniform Resource Locator (same thing as a Web address).
Visual Basic	Microsoft's applet development language.
VRML	Virtual Reality Modeling Language. A Web protocol for describing 3-dimensional spaces and enabling specialized Web browsers to view and "fly through" or "walk around" them.

Table 2.1 Some Web Terms You Should Know *(continued)*

WHAT'S YOUR BUDGET?

The type of Web site you build will depend to some extent on your budget. This is a similar issue to that of choosing an e-mail connection for a company or institution. One can have an e-mail system with a gateway to the Net (which is like saying that you can get to the freeway but you don't live close to the freeway) or one's network can be "on the Net." Even with direct Net connections there are levels—ISDN, T1, T3 etc.—each of which have different price points for telephone and Internet service. Similarly, to have a Web site, you can obtain access to an existing Web server (through a service provider), or you can set up your own server. If you set up your own (you can do this by purchasing a new computer or adapting an existing one), you can decide what platform to do it on and with what speed, what "size of pipe," and what connection. (Chapter 13 talks about different types of Web servers.)

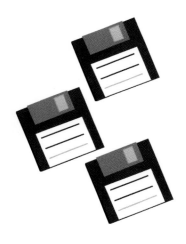

WHO'S GOING TO DO THE WORK?

This book will enable you to do it all yourself, if you're so inclined. If all you want to do is assemble a basic Web site, then you'll have no problem following along with this book to do so. If you have greater ambitions, such as incorporating various media into your site or building in interactivity, this book will help you figure out how to do so, but you'll have to rely on your own skills or ability to learn to master some of the related technologies.

For a large-scale site or one for a business entity, you might very well not want to do all the work yourself. If you want action at your site, you'll probably want to find a programmer to write the programs, applets, or scripts. If you want a sophisticated graphical design, you'd be best off hiring a good designer whose work you admire and telling her what you want. I (Christian) paint and draw and I play around a little with computer art tools, but when my company needed a logo and some graphical elements for our Web site, we hired a designer whose work we'd seen and liked on the Net to produce those items for us.

So even if you don't plan to do it all yourself, this book will help you figure out which parts of the job to take on yourself and which you'll want to find a consultant to help you with. Even if you put together the site yourself, initially, you also have to consider the issue of maintenance. How often will the site be updated? Will it have to be redesigned from time to time? Who's going to respond to the e-mail traffic it generates? Who will be in charge of fixing the typos when they're noticed?

WHO'S YOUR AUDIENCE?

When planning a Web site, you need to think carefully about who your audience is. Who are the users you expect to connect to your site and what will they be looking for when they get there? Right now, we're designing a Web site for an academic department. They came to us with a clear idea of the three different groups in their audience: potential grad students interested in applying to the department; academics interested in the department's research; and companies interested in joint projects with the department. The site's home page will have to welcome all three and steer them toward the pages and content they may be interested in. These can overlap as well. The design need not be linear, as in a pamphlet or book.

So for a company, think about who the site is for. Your customers? Your vendors? Your clients? What are the needs of those users? How can you supplement the ways you already serve them?

CONTENT—WHO NEEDS IT?

A lot of the Web is all flash and very little content. It's important that you have the graphic design values (or "production values") appropriate for the image of your company, but if the substance is not there, no one will stay. One problem with the traditional advertising model is that advertisements can easily be ignored on the Web. This fact forces you to integrate your promotional information with substantial and intriguing content. If you want someone to fill out a form, you may have to offer them some sort of incentive, such as a prize or discount.

It's natural to think in terms of the content you have lying around (press releases—the Web is already choked with them), and some of that will be appropriate, such as annual reports, articles, and so on, but be prepared to develop new content especially for the Web site.

habits & strategies

One typical gambit to bring "traffic" to a commercial Web site is to include some useful information or up-to-date set of links.

Don't cut corners: hire professionals or use in-house writers, editors, designers, and programmers.

DESIGN FOR A NEW MEDIUM

The look of a Web site is as important as the look of print publications, but some of the issues are different. Consult professionals who know something about the medium. You can reuse much of your existing camera-ready art (logos, glossy photos, and so on—see Chapter 8 for more on graphics), but text will effectively have to be re-"typeset" as part of the HTML design. Existing text files are useful, though (and even documents that only exist on paper can be scanned, put through a character-recognition program, and then converted to HTML).

Part of designing a coherent site is establishing a consistent "look" for all your pages. Just like a print publication will have an in-house style sheet and a basic design for all its pages, you need to approach your online publication the same way. The Web is very fluid and people don't always know when they've left one site and entered another. It helps to clearly label the pages of your site, and because people still don't always see or read the "road signs," a consistent look can help to bind the entire site together in your user's mind.

When designing a site, take into account the entire range of bandwidths your users might rely on to connect to your site. If you have a flashy, graphics-heavy home page at your site, consider setting up a text-only alternative for people with very slow connections.

One other sense of design on the Web is "hypertext design," the way the different elements of the site link to each other. Hypertext (or hypermedia) organization need not be linear (although there may be a linear "path" through the site). Instead, connections should be well planned and seem intuitive to the user. They should also be consistent throughout the site, so users will know what to expect.

Site navigation is another important element of Web-site design. Users should always be able to return to the home page, to other index pages, or to a search page if there is one. Simple text links can provide this service, but flashier methods, such as navigation bars and image maps, have become almost de rigeur (see Chapters 8 and 12 for more on graphical links and image maps).

CAUTION

You should also consider having some sort of copyright statement, possibly on every page or in one central place but linked from every page, to make it clear who owns the contents of your site and what restrictions you want to put on the reuse of any of the contents, written or graphical.

Whenever you see a Web site with a design you like, or for which you're curious about the underlying HTML source file, use your browser's View Source command to see how the page was done for yourself (see Figure 2.6).

OTHER THINGS TO THINK ABOUT AHEAD OF TIME

All of the ideas covered in this section are dealt with at length, in the appropriate part of the book. Here at the beginning of the process, though, you should take a moment to think ahead about these topics. You may save yourself trouble and grief later by doing a little planning now.

Commerce—Doing Business on the Web

If you'll be selling anything on the Web, how will you make the transactions? You'll need to reassure your customers about security. You'll need to use a Web server whose security is robust enough for commerce. See Chapter 13 for more details.

habits & strategies

Think in terms of your site's "front end" and "back end." The front end is the visible appearance of the site. The back end is the stuff that makes it work—everything from the server to the scripts and routines that create interaction. Most of the book focuses on front-end issues, but they are not entirely separable.

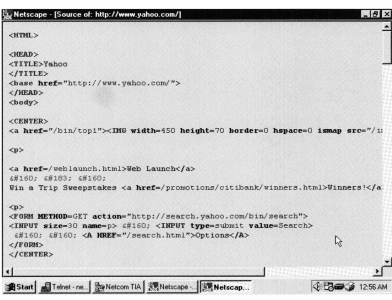

Figure 2.6 The top of the source document for the popular Yahoo directory's home page.

trends

Chapter 13 will discuss the range of possibilities currently available for making secure transactions and reassuring your customers that their credit card or other information will be kept confidential and out of the eyes of snoops. But in the near future, these issues may be solved in a more broad way, as protocols for secure HTTP transfers become more widely accepted and implemented.

A Picture's Worth a Thousand Bytes

A credible Web site must have decent graphics. Standards are still evolving for images (different browsers can handle different types). Images take up much more bandwidth than text, so efficient use of images is important. Do not clutter up the main page, as it will make users impatient. Use thumbnails (miniature images) linked to larger sized images when possible. JPEGs (compressed graphics files with the extension .jpg) are often the best choice nowadays. You'll need to be able to convert from one graphics format to another (we'll recommend a few conversion tools). If you're working with a professional designer, that person may have these issues covered. Chapter 8 has the straight skinny on graphics.

Multimedia—Lights, Camera, Action!

Web sites are almost always expected to make use of as many different types of media as possible. This includes such formats as sounds, video, and animation. The latest Web browsers can accommodate special "plug-ins," such as Macromedia's "Shockwave" Director plug-in and Adobe's "Amber" Acrobat plug-in, that enable them to play other multimedia file formats. All of these media require higher bandwidth than what even a fast modem can provide to be practical, but they are becoming more and more important in attracting people to your site. (See Chapter 9 for more on other media.

Scripts and Automated Routines

If you want the site to "do" anything besides just send flat documents out, you will have to put together a set of scripts. Scripting is a very rudimentary form of programming, similar to macro recording. Examples of script uses include forms, such as guestbooks and search pages. There is a standard method for linking Web client events to pre-scripted actions at the server end, called CGI (see Chapter 2), for which all sorts of routines can be found and/or cannibalized for free from the Net. A new scripting language called JavaScript should make it easy for non-programmers to link together normal Web documents with plug-in applets and scripted routines. More sophisticated uses will require professionals or someone with the time and resources to learn.

CROSS-LINKING TO THE REST OF THE NET

Once a site is set up, you need to put out the word to bring visitors (also called "hits" on the server). Being part of the Web means creating links to other related sites and attempting to have such sites include links back to you. You don't want your site to end up as a detached island. (See Chapter 13 for how to promote your site.)

PLAN NOW FOR THE GROWTH OF YOUR SITE

Web sites should not be static. The Web is littered with moribund sites whose creators have stopped maintaining them. (Our technical editor tells us that some people refer to such dead or dying sites as "cobwebs.") The visitors slow eventually to a trickle. A site should have a "what's new" area for announcements, and good Web design will make changing or updating the site easier. Use the hierarchical file structure wisely and write clean HTML documents so others can make changes in the future.

WHAT'S NEXT?

The next six chapters (3 through 8) cover the essentials of HTML—the building-block language of the Web—both for document design and for creating hypertext links. It's much easier than you think, especially using Netscape Editor. Just read through Chapter 4 only, and you've already learned enough to put together a credible home page. You can try making an internal Web site available only on your local network or even just your computer if you want to practice any of these techniques.

The four chapters after that (9 through 12) explain how to integrate other media into your site and develop more advanced inter- activity. Chapter 13 covers how to find a server, publish your pages, and promote your site.

After you've read the first eight chapters, skip around. Read as much or as little as you need, and save the rest for later, if ever. We know you've got more important things to do!

How HTML Works

43

FAST FORWARD

```
<TR>
    <TD></TD>
    <TD align=center><img
    <TD></TD>
    <TD></TD>
</TR>
</TABLE>
```

WHAT IS HTML? ➤ *pp. 46-48*

- HTML stands for hypertext markup language.
- HTML is a set of codes that instructs a Web browser both how to display a document and what to do when "hot" links are selected (or clicked).
- HTML describes how a document is structured, not precisely how it should be displayed, so different programs running on different types of computers handle the same HTML codes differently but are still faithful to the intentions behind the codes.
- There are several different versions of HTML, most notably HTML 2.0 (the most commonly "understood" version), Netscape extensions to HTML, and HTML 3.2 (which is still in the works).

```
<html>
<head>
    <title>Essential HTML Tags</title>
</head>
<body>
Should a body meet a body coming through
</body>
</html>
```

ALL HTML DOCUMENTS MUST HAVE ➤ *pp. 49-52*

1. <HTML> at the beginning and </HTML> at the end
2. A head, beginning with <HEAD>, containing a title (surrounded by <TITLE> and </TITLE>), and ending with </HEAD>
3. A body, beginning with <BODY> and ending with </BODY>

```
<h1>H1 -- The Most Important Head
<h2>H2 -- Major Subheadings</h2>
<h3>H3 -- Subsubheadings</h3>
<h4>H4 -- Sub sub sub headings</h
<h5>H5 -- Sub sub sub sub heading
<h6>H6 -- The lowest heading leve
```

HTML TAGS THAT STRUCTURE DOCUMENTS INCLUDE ➤ *pp. 52-54*

1. Headings (<H1> ... </H1> through <H6> ... </H6>)
2. Paragraph (<P>)
3. Line break (<BR>)
4. Horizontal rule (<HR>)

```
This word is <i>italicized</i>
and this one is <b>bold</b>.
```

HTML TAGS THAT FORMAT TEXT INCLUDE ➤ *pp. 54-58*

1. Logical formatting tags, such as emphasis (<EM> ... </EM>)
2. Physical formatting tags, such as bold (<B> ... </B>) and italics (<I> ... </I>)
3. Netscape-only font size tags (<FONT SIZE=*n*>)
4. Preformatted text (<PRE> ... </PRE>)

```
<ul>
<li>Levi Asher's seminal <a href="http://
Kicks</a></li>

<li>What little we know about <a href="ht

<li>Just what is <a href="http://hyperfuz

<li>They call it <a href="http://adaweb.c

<li>Memes and voices from <a href="http:/
</ul>
```

```
          <a href="http://
```

```
<p>&lt; (less than)</p>

<p>&gt; (greater than)</p>

<p>&quot; (quotation mark)</p>

<p>&amp; (ampersand)</p>
```

HTML TAGS THAT MAKE LISTS INCLUDE ➤ *pp. 58-60*

- Ordered lists (<OL> ... </OL>, each item starting with <LI>)
- Unordered lists (<UL> ... </UL>, each item starting with <LI>)
- Definition lists (<DL> ... </DL>, each term starting with <DT> and each definition starting with <DD>)

HTML TAGS FOR HYPERLINKS INCLUDE ➤ *p. 61*

- Links to external Web documents (<A HREF="*url*"> ... </A>)
- Links to named text in the current document (<A HREF="*name*"> ... </A>)
- Links to named text in external Web documents (<A HREF="*url#name*"> ... </A>)
- Links to other objects (<A HREF="*filename*"> ... </A>)

SPECIAL CHARACTERS CAN BE CODED WITH ➤ *pp. 62-63*

Codes that start with an ampersand and end with a semicolon, such as

- < for <
- > for >
- " for " *and*
- & for &

ONLINE HTML REFERENCES CAN BE FOUND AT ➤ *p. 63*

- **http://developer.netscape.com/platform/ html_compilation/index.html**
- **http://www.ncsa.uiuc.edu/demoweb/ html-primer.html**
- **http://kuhttp.cc.ukans.edu/lynx_help/ HTML_quick.html**
- **http://www.access.digex.net/~werbach/ barebone.html**
- **http://www.cs.cmu.edu/~tilt/cgh/**
- **http://limestone.kosone.com/people/nelson/nl.htm**

HTML documents are the building blocks of every Web site. There are good, sound reasons why you should learn the broad outlines of HTML before you proceed further. HTML is the language that makes HTML documents look and behave the way they do on the Web.

With a Web-publishing program like Netscape Editor, you don't have to "dirty your hands" typing in HTML codes, but by being aware of HTML and how it works, you get a clearer idea of what Netscape is really doing when you edit and format your documents.

After this chapter, we won't generally speak in terms of HTML codes or inserting tags or anything like that. Instead, we'll focus on the result (the "effect") and how to accomplish it in Netscape. We'll leave all the theory and "coding" behind. Meanwhile, this chapter will give you a background in HTML and help you understand why Web documents look the way they do and why some designs are possible and others aren't.

WHAT'S HTML?

HTML stands for *hypertext markup language.* It is a computer language (but not a *programming* language, if you care) that controls the appearance and behavior of Web documents.

HTML provides a set of codes. When these codes are inserted into a text document, they instruct Web browsers both how to display the document and what to do when "hot" links are selected (or clicked). HTML describes how a document is structured, not precisely how it should be displayed. Because HTML deals with structure instead of appearances, different programs running on different types of computers handle the same HTML codes differently, but they do so in a manner that is consistent with the intentions behind the codes.

If you've looked at the underlying source of an existing Web page, you already have an idea of what HTML documents looks like. (To see the underlying source of a Web page in most browsers, select View I Source *or* Source Document, or something similar; some browsers use a Save as HTML command.)

Then again, did you always do the reading for all of your classes in school? If you're too busy to delay starting your project any longer, jump ahead to Chapter 4.

**h a b i t s &
s t r a t e g i e s**

Remember to peek behind the curtain any time you see a Web page you really like. You can even copy HTML coding examples from existing pages and adapt them for your own documents.

HTML documents consist of plain text mixed with codes. At first, source documents are hard to interpret, but you soon get used to distinguishing the coded tags from the regular text.

An Example

Here's an example of something that looks simple in a browser window (and is easy to create with Netscape Editor, by the way), but might seem very complicated if you were to type it in yourself. Imagine a section of a Web document that features links to other related sites on the Web. It would start with a heading, have some explanatory text, and then start listing or discussing the sites. An HTML document that presents that material would look something like this:

Other Related Sites

Here are some other sites on the Web you might be interested in:

- Levi Asher's seminal Literary Kicks
- What little we know about antiweb
- Just what is Hyperfuzzy?
- They call it adaweb
- Memes and voices from World 3

The </li> tags at the end of each line in this list are optional and are, in fact, usually left out.

The underlying HTML used to create that effect (as produced by Netscape) would look like this:

```
<h2>Other Related Sites</h2>
<p>Here are some other sites on the Web you might be interested in:</p>
<ul>
<li>Levi Asher's seminal <a href="http://www.charm.net/~brooklyn">Literary
Kicks</a></li>
<li>What little we know about <a
href="http://www.emf.net/~mal/antiweb.html">antiweb</a></li>
<li>Just what is <a href="http://hyperfuzzy.com">Hyperfuzzy?</a></li>
<li>They call it <a href="http://adaweb.com">adaweb</a></li>
<li>Memes and voices from <a href="http://www.world3.com">World 3</a></li>
</ul>
```

Understanding HTML codes gets a little easier after a while. Nevertheless, you shouldn't feel like you're missing out on anything all that great if you avoid dealing with HTML directly.

More than One Kind of HTML

In this and later chapters, I will cover variations of HTML, including HTML 2.0 (the most widely accepted standard), the set of Netscape HTML extensions (which are now widely accepted as well as easy to take advantage of with Navigator Gold), HTML 3.2 (which is still being developed but is partially understood by Navigator), and extensions for specific browsers (namely Microsoft Internet Explorer).

Platform-Independent Design

The Web is designed to be a "platform-independent" medium. That means users should be able to view the content on the Web no matter what type of computer, operating system, or Web browser they use. When designing a Web document or site, you have to consider your likely audience, what computers you expect it to use, and what Web browsers you expect it to use. You can optimize a page so that it looks best in Netscape Navigator, but then people using other browsers may not see things the same way. It's usually a good idea to make sure that text-only browsers get something worthwhile, too. We recommend designing for the broadest possible audience, but who you design for is up to you.

CAUTION

It's tempting sometimes to use tags in ways that are technically incorrect to achieve effects such as indentation. One of the risks of doing this is that a browser may interpret your unorthodox formatting unpredictably. Just because Netscape indents lists, for example, don't assume that all browsers will.

trends

As browsers become more sophisticated and the Internet keeps getting more popular, some people think that users in the future will spend most of their time using Web browser/Internet client programs such as Netscape for most of their daily computer activities. Others think that the Internet/browser features will be integrated into computer operating systems, rendering browser programs obsolete.

If you ever find yourself typing in a tag by hand, consider using uppercase characters. They take a little longer to type (it adds up!), but they stand out much better and make it easier to "read" HTML code.

HTML TAGS

Most of the codes used in HTML are *tags*. A tag marks adjacent or surrounded text and tells Web browsers how to handle the text. In this section, we'll explain the most common HTML tags. Without having to learn all the specific tags, you'll then have an idea of the building blocks of HTML documents and what is possible on the Web.

Tags and Angle Brackets

HTML documents are composed of plain ASCII text. Your computer can display and you can type ASCII text from your keyboard. The controlling HTML codes are referred to as tags. Tags appear between angle brackets, the < and > that are also called less-than and greater-than signs. Tags are not case-sensitive, so you can type them with upper- or lowercase letters. For example, both <p> and <P> have the same effect: they indicate the start of a new paragraph.

Most Tags Mark Text by Surrounding It

Most tags occur in pairs and surround the text they affect. For example, here's a portion of an HTML source document:

```
To make a word appear <B>darker</B> and more prominent, you can surround it
with the HTML bold tag.
```

And here's what the document looks like when it is viewed with a Web browser:

To make a word appear **darker** and more prominent, you can surround it with the HTML bold tag.

Skip ahead to Chapter 4 if you've learned all you want to know about HTML and would like to get started on a document.

The <B> tag before the word *darker* applies boldface to the word. The </B> tag indicates the end of the boldfacing.

Some tags, most notably the line break tag, don't surround text. But for the most part, HTML tags occur in pairs.

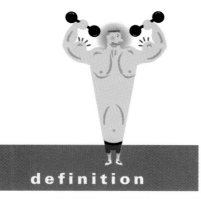

definition

ASCII: *A standard set of 128 characters (mostly keyboard, international, and symbol characters) that just about every computer can display correctly.*

The Special Comment Tag

HTML documents can contain comments, enclosed in special tags, where you can leave notes to yourself or others about your Web site. Special comment tags start with <!-- (less-than, exclamation point, hyphen, hyphen) and end with --> (hyphen, hyphen, greater-than), as in this example:

```
<!—A browser will ignore this text, but you can
leave messages for yourself or others in the
source document with this comment tag.—>
```

Housekeeping Codes

Many documents on the Web are created by computer programs or are created with certain types of indexing and interpreting programs in mind. To satisfy these program and indexing requirements, every document must follow standard rules about how HTML documents start and end and what sort of information they provide.

"Required" Header Codes

A couple of tags are considered mandatory in every HTML document. As long as you use a program like Navigator to create HTML documents, these tags are inserted into your document automatically.

First of all, every HTML document must start with

```
<HTML>
```

and end with

```
</HTML>
```

In addition to the HTML beginning and ending codes that surround the rest of its contents, each Web document must also have a head and a body.

CAUTION

You can use comment tags to temporarily disable a portion of an HTML document, but some browsers choke on any codes (especially angle brackets) inside comments, although they shouldn't (they should ignore them). To be safe, you can change all <> to {} or some alternative punctuation marks (inside a comment).

Just after the <HTML> tag, a Web document should contain a head section, starting with

```
<HEAD>
```

and ending with

```
</HEAD>
```

The purpose of the HEAD section of the document is to provide supplementary information that isn't displayed in the browser window. Although various advanced codes are allowed between the HEAD codes, the only imperative thing to have inside a HEAD section is the document's title. The title itself must be enclosed between

```
<TITLE>
```

and

```
</TITLE>
```

The text between these two tags appears in the title bar of graphical browsers and somewhere prominent on the screen of character-based browsers. It's also the name of the document as far as the Web is concerned. If anyone adds a bookmark to your page, the title text is what appears on the bookmark menu. The head and title tags can all be run together on a line (in fact, no paragraph breaks are required in HTML—they're used only for legibility):

```
<HEAD><TITLE>A "Tidy" Web Page</TITLE></HEAD>
```

Some of the advanced design features, such as background wallpaper or color on a page, are associated with the <BODY> tag in HTML.

After the head comes the body. The remaining contents of the document fits between the starting and ending body tags, which, as you might imagine, are

```
<BODY>
```

and

```
</BODY>
```

Once you've got <HTML><HEAD><TITLE>*Your Title Here*</TITLE></HEAD><BODY> at the beginning and </BODY></HTML> tags at the end of your document, you can actually go ahead and format the contents between the two body tags.

Recommended Footer Codes

The surrounding HTML, HEAD, BODY, and TITLE pairs help browser software interpret documents and make it easier for other programs and machines to keep track of the information on the Web. There is also a tradition of sorts about what to put on each Web page for the sake of the *people* reading it. Besides the obvious things, such as a title, it's recommended that the person responsible for the document sign or initial the page at the bottom (that is, type his or her name, initials, or e-mail address). A pair of tags, <ADDRESS> and </ADDRESS>, are provided for surrounding and marking that type of information. Some people also recommend including the date that the document was last modified.

If you are posting information for which you hold the copyright, you should probably put a standard copyright statement on each page or perhaps each major page. There are no special tags for date and copyright statements.

Tags for Structuring a Document

A number of basic HTML tags are used to control the structure of a document. They range from a hierarchy of heading levels, through tags used to break lines of text, start new paragraphs, and insert horizontal lines (rules) to tags used to create lists. What these tags have in common is that they describe conceptual relationships between the parts of a document. For example, the third-level heading starts a section subordinate to the second, and the list items constitute a sequence of steps or a list of equivalent choices. Different browsers may render the text slightly differently, but the intention symbolized by the code will be clear no matter what.

Heading Levels 1 through 6

There are six heading levels, H1 through H6. Each heading level does not display text at a specific size or in a particular alignment, but you can reasonably expect each heading level to display text smaller than the preceding level. It is traditional to use only one H1 heading in a document, at the beginning (often the H1 heading is a restatement of the title text), but using a single H1 heading is not a hard-and-fast rule. Figure 3.1 shows all six heading levels in Netscape.

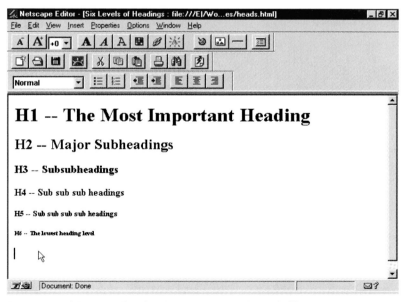

Figure 3.1 All six heading levels as they're rendered in Netscape

The underlying code for those headers looks like this:

```
<body>

<h1>H1 -- The Most Important Heading</h1>

<h2>H2 -- Major Subheadings</h2>

<h3>H3 -- Subsubheadings</h3>

<h4>H4 -- Sub sub sub headings</h4>

<h5>H5 -- Sub sub sub sub headings</h5>

<h6>H6 -- The lowest heading level</h6>
```

Paragraph and Line Breaks

Paragraphs are preceded by <P> and followed by </P> (the closing </P> is optional in HTML 2.0). The paragraph is the most basic (or "normal") unit of text.

A line break (starting a new line of text without starting a new paragraph) is indicated by a single <BR> tag. BR has no closing tag.

Horizontal Rules, or Lines

Another way to structure a document is to separate its sections by inserting horizontal lines, or rules. The tag for a horizontal rule is <HR>. (<HR> is another non-paired tag.) Figure 3.2 shows how a horizontal rule looks.

Formatting Text

As with word processing documents, text formats in HTML documents can be used to help clarify meaning and provide emphasis.

There are two types of text-formatting tags in HTML, logical and physical. *Logical tags* define the meaning or purpose of the affected text. *Physical tags* control the exact appearance of the text. Whenever possible, using logical tags is recommended. Logical tags let individual browsers determine the best way to achieve the intended result. In most browsers, for example, the <EM> (emphasis) tag and the <I> (italics) tag produce the same result. But a browser that "reads" text out loud to those with sight limitations might interpret <EM> as a slight increase in volume and interpret <I> as a change in intonation or ignore it completely.

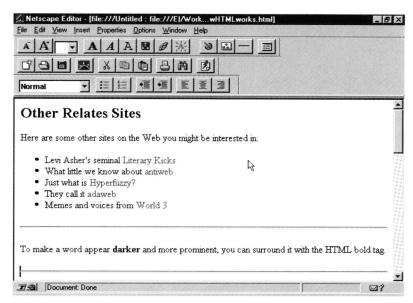

Figure 3.2 An <HR> tag inserts a horizontal line into a document

There is also something called "preformatted text." It must appear exactly as is and is not meant to be interpreted at all by a Web browser. Preformatted text is explained a few pages later in this chapter.

CAUTION

Netscape Editor changes most logical tags to physical tags that are often displayed similarly. It changes <EM> to <i>, <STRONG> to <b>, and <CITE> to <i>, for example, without even asking.

Logical Formatting Tags

Only a handful of logical formatting tags are available in HTML 2.0. Two deal with emphasis and a few others describe the meaning or context of the affected text.

Two logical tags are available for indicating emphasis. Regular emphasis is applied by surrounding text with <EM> and </EM>. These codes, in graphical browsers at least, are usually rendered as italics. Extra emphasis is applied with <STRONG> and </STRONG>. Usually these codes are rendered as boldface.

In print publications names of publications are typically set in italics, but you can leave the decision of how to set publication names to the browser by surrounding publication names with <CITE> and </CITE>. Addresses can be indicated with <ADDRESS> and </AD-DRESS>. (The address tag is often used to mark the name or e-mail address of the creator of a Web page.) Stretches of programming code or output from a computer screen can be indicated with <CODE> and </CODE>, usually rendered in a typewriter font.

When quoting more than four lines or so of a source, it's customary to set off the quotation from regular text. In HTML, you do this with the <BLOCKQUOTE> and </BLOCKQUOTE> tags. Most browsers indent from both the left and right margins to indicate a quotation. Consider the following code and how it is rendered in the next illustration.

```
<BLOCKQUOTE>
It was doubly odd to be engaged in trivial calculations based on a series of
radio pulses believed to have been transmitted by living things in another
part of the galaxy and to reflect, in such circumstances, on a man whose
genius had been acclaimed by Napoleon but who was drawn into star-ponds of
such inertia that he left his greatest work unopened on his desk for two full
years.
</BLOCKQUOTE>
```

This sums up how I sometimes feel about my work:

> It was doubly odd to be engaged in trivial calculations based on a series of radio pulses believed to have been transmitted by living things in another part of the galaxy and to reflect, in such circumstances, on a man whose genius had been acclaimed by Napoleon but who was drawn into star-ponds of such inertia that he left his greatest work unopened on his desk for two full years.

That about says it, eh?

HTML 3.2 and later versions introduce a different set of tags entirely for block quotations. Tags are started and ended with <BQ> and </BQ>. Quotations are attributed using the <CREDIT> and </CREDIT> tags (usually at the end of the quotation), as shown:

```
years.
<CREDIT>Don DeLillo, <CITE>Ratner's Star</CITE></CREDIT>
</BQ>
```

By the way, HTML 3.2 also provides a tag for normal (short) quotations, <Q> and </Q>. This tag can be used instead of quotation

habits & strategies

Official specifications for HTML 2.0 don't include underlining tags (because links are usually underlined by default and underlined text could confuse readers), although browsers do interpret <U> and </U> as beginning and ending tags for underlined text. If you use these tags, remember that they will not necessarily be supported for all readers.

marks. The benefit of this tag over the quotation mark special character is that it can be rendered as whatever character is appropriate in the language of the user. (However, you must set the language for the document by using the <LANG> code, and that's a whole other story.)

Physical Formatting Tags

Physical tags are best used when you want exact control over the appearance of text. Basic HTML 2.0 includes only a small list of tags, but HTML 3.2 introduces a few more.

To make text bold, surround it with <B> and </B>. To italicize text, surround it with <I> and </I>. To format text in a typewriter font (often some variation of Courier), surround it with <TT> and </TT> (TT stands for teletype, an archaic computer term). Most browsers display their "typewriter" or monospaced font in a slightly smaller size than they do normal, variable-width fonts (usually 10 points versus 12). Why? We don't know.

In theory, publications for the Web are created without concern about the ultimate appearance of the document. In reality, people who publish on the Web usually want a little more control over the appearance of text. Netscape introduced some additional codes for just that purpose, and many of them are supported by competing Web browsers, even if they aren't part of the official HTML specifications. The Netscape tag that controls the appearance of text is called <FONT> and currently it's only official command is SIZE=n. The value of n can range from 1 to 7. To set text to size 5, for example, put <FONT SIZE=5> before the text and </FONT> afterward. Newer FONT options include commands that control the color of text and even the specific typeface to use.

In the Netscape scheme, there is a base font size, which by default is 3. Headings and other special elements are considered to be larger or smaller than that base font size by some number of units. The size of text can be set relative to the base font size by setting SIZE equal to +n or −n. For example, to make text larger than its base font size by 2 units, surround it with <FONT SIZE=+2> and </FONT>.

You can change the base font size for a document with a tag called (surprise) <BASEFONT SIZE=n>. As with the <FONT SIZE=n> tag, n can range from 1 to 7.

Some use the <PRE> tag to get precise control over the appearance of text on the screen. The trade-off is that text appears in a typewriter font (with same-width characters and spaces).

Preformatted Text

When portions of text must appear exactly as is and should not be interpreted at all by a Web browser (that is, no words should be wrapped, no line breaks inserted), such text can be coded as preformatted text. Preformatted text is surrounded by the tags <PRE> and </PRE>. It appears in a monospaced font with line breaks appearing exactly (and only) where typed. If a line is too long to fit on a browser screen, it disappears off the edge of the screen without being wrapped to the line below. (If the goal is merely to indicate typewritten text or lines of programming code, there are two tags for that purpose, neither of which controls the text layout as strictly as <PRE>. Both are explained in the upcoming section.)

Unlike all other HTML coding, preformatted text displays spaces, tabs, and line breaks exactly as typed, so it can be used to lay out text when the characters' positions relative to each other are significant (as is the case with some poetry, for example).

Organizing Information with Lists

Lists are useful for communicating complicated information in a succinct, structured way. HTML allows for three kinds of lists (well, it allows for a few others as well, but only three useful kinds). HTML offers ordered (numbered) lists, unordered (bulleted) lists, and definition lists. Definition lists consist of definition terms and their definitions.

Typically, ordered and unordered lists are indented from the left margin (or from the most recent indentation) and definitions are indented from the position of the definition terms, but how lists are indented varies from browser to browser.

It's possible to nest lists (that is, to put one list inside another) as long as the tags are kept straight. When HTML 3.2 becomes standard, it will be possible to give any list a heading with the <LH> (list heading) tag.

Ordered (Numbered) Lists

To make a numbered list, you don't actually type any numbers. Instead, you surround the list with <OL> and </OL> (ordered list) and then you

CAUTION

It's tempting to use list starting and ending tags to (improperly) force indentation, since many browsers interpret the tags that way, but you do run the risk that other browsers might interpret them differently. Basic HTML (3.2) doesn't have an established way to indent text, but HTML 3.0 and later includes horizontal tabs.

start each new item on the list with <LI> (list item), as in the following example:

```
<OL>
<LI>Lather.
<LI>Rinse.
<LI>Repeat.
</OL>
```

This list will be rendered as shown:

1. Lather.
2. Rinse.
3. Repeat.

List numbering is handled automatically by the browser. If you edit the list and, say, rearrange its items, the items are renumbered automatically (one of the great advantages of coded lists).

Unordered (Bulleted) Lists

To make a bulleted list, you don't actually type any bullet symbols. Instead, you surround the list with <UL> and </UL> (unordered list) and then you start each new item on the list with <LI> (list item), as in the following example:

```
<UL>
<LI>Lies
<LI>Damned Lies
<LI>Statistics
</UL>
```

This list will be rendered as shown:

- Lies
- Damned Lies
- Statistics

In nested bulleted lists, each subsequent list is indented further and uses a different bullet character. For example, the following tag renders the list shown in the illustration below:

```
<UL>
<LI>Lies
<LI>Damned Lies
<LI>Statistics
<UL>
<LI>Government Statistics
<LI>Private-research Statistics
<LI>Made-up Statistics
</UL>
</UL>
```

- Lies
- Damned Lies
- Statistics
  - ☐ Government Statistics
  - ☐ Private-research Statistics
  - ☐ Made-up Statistics

Definition Lists

A definition list is a list of terms and their definitions, as in a glossary. To make a definition list, start and end with <DL> and </DL>. For each entry, insert <DT> before the term to be defined and <DD> before the definition. Here's an example:

```
<DL>
<DT>Doe
<DD>A deer (a female deer)
</DL>
```

In Netscape, this definition list is rendered like so:

Doe
    A deer (a female deer)

Advanced Layout (Tables and Frames)

Although HTML was developed to communicate content and structure at the expense of specific visual layouts, tags were inevitably introduced to help with the organization and layout of pages. Both HTML 3.0 and the Netscape extensions specify tags for tables. Table tags are somewhat complicated to enter by hand but are as easy as making a table in a word processor if you use the right tool. (Later versions of Navigator Gold should include a table editor.) Tables make it possible to lay elements side by side or make complicated layouts.

A newer feature is *frames*. Frames break the browser window into areas that users can scroll. They can even link to additional pages separately. Frames, like tables, are very difficult to code by hand. Although they are easy to set up using a special tool, making them work properly can be tricky, and the jury is still out about whether frames make Web sites easier to navigate or whether they make Web pages ugly, clunky, and complicated.

Tables are covered in Chapter 10; frames in Chapter 12.

Hyperlinks (Hypertext and Hypermedia Links)

The other major type of HTML tag is the *anchor tag*. Anchor tags are used to create hyperlinks. All opening anchor tags start with <A and all closing anchor tags are simply </A>. Anchors can do the following:

- Link to other documents (the most common type of link) in the form <A HREF="*url*">
- Link to a named text segment of the current document in the form <A HREF="#*name*">
- Link to a named segment of another document in the form <A HREF="*url*#*name*">
- Link to other (non-Web document) objects in the form <A HREF="*filename*">

Don't worry if this makes no sense at all. Hyperlinks are covered in great detail in Chapter 7.

Links help make Web sites coherent and provide organizational structure and navigational aids to the reader. Besides highlighting keywords as hypertext links, you can also embed graphical links into documents and create "image maps." Image maps send the reader to different destinations depending on where the map is clicked.

habits & strategies

Netscape Editor automatically converts reserved characters to their HTML equivalents as you type (without making a big deal out of it), so you've got this covered.

Reserved and Special Characters

Because HTML codes make special use of some of the basic characters (such as < and >, as you've already seen), you run into a problem if you ever try to use those characters in an HTML document. Characters used in tags confuse and distract the browser program. They cause it to choke on the document and display it incorrectly. All reserved characters (along with a large set of special characters, including those you can't type on your keyboard such as <UNKNOWN SYMBOL>) can be represented in HTML by special codes starting with & (ampersand) and ending with ; (semicolon). For example, the code for < (the less-than sign) is < (the *lt* stands for less-than). Because " (the quotation mark) is used to set off file names and & (the ampersand) is used for the special-character codes, both of them have their own codes (" and &, respectively).

Table 3.1 shows a list of some of the common special characters and the HTML coding needed to produce them.

Special Character	HTML Coding
<	&lt;
>	&gt;
&	&amp;
"	&quot;
©	&copy;
®	&reg;
™	&tm;

Table 3.1 HMTL codes for Special Characters

Not all special character codes are recognized by all browsers. For example, many browsers still don't recognize the © code for ©.

CAUTION

Special character entity codes are the only case-sensitive codes. For example, é is the code for a lowercase e with an acute accent on it, but É is the code for an uppercase E with an acute accent.

bookmark

For a complete list of the special characters and codes to create them, see http://www.sandia.gov/sci_compute/symbols.html.

ONLINE HTML REFERENCES

For more information about HTML, check out these online references:

- The HTML Language Specification
  **(http://developer.netscape.com/platform/
  html_compilation/index.html)**
- The Beginner's Guide to HTML
  (http://www.ncsa.uiuc.edu/demoweb/html-primer.html)
- HTML Quick Reference
  (http://kuhttp.cc.ukans.edu/lynx_help/HTML_quick.html)
- Bare Bones HTML
  (http://www.access.digex.net/~werbach/barebone.html)
- Composing good HTML
  (http://www.cs.cmu.edu/~tilt/cgh/)
- The WEB DESIGNER
  (http://limestone.kosone.com/people/nelson/nl.htm)

Remember also to view the source of Web pages whose formatting you would like to imitate.

Now it's time to build your Web site!

Starting an HTML Document

Your Page

_____

_____

ASSISTANCE

NETSCAPE WEB PAGE TEMPLATES

Edit

FAST FORWARD

MAKE A HOME PAGE WITH THE NETSCAPE WIZARD ➤ *pp. 70-79*

1. Select File I New Document I From Wizard.
2. Fill out the Web-design form.
3. Click the Create Page button.
4. Click Edit, Save, and OK.
5. Save your new home page.

USE A NETSCAPE HOME PAGE TEMPLATE ➤ *pp. 79-82*

1. Select File I New Document I From Template.
2. Choose a Template.
3. Click Edit, Save, and OK.
4. Edit and customize the template.

DOWNLOAD AND EDIT A DOCUMENT FROM THE WEB ➤ *pp. 82-83*

1. Browse your way to the page you want to copy.
2. Click Edit, Save, and OK.
3. Edit and customize the copied document.

START A BLANK WEB DOCUMENT ➤ *p. 83*

1. Select File I New Document I Blank.
2. Start typing and formatting your new document.

File

New Web Browser	Ctrl+N
New Document	▶
Edit Document	
New Mail Message	Ctrl+M
Mail Document...	
Open Location...	Ctrl+L
Open File in Browser...	Ctrl+O
Open File in Editor...	
Save As...	
Upload File...	
Page Setup...	
Print...	
Print Preview	
Close	Ctrl+W
Exit	

Blank
From Template
From Wizard...

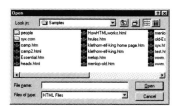

OPEN AN EXISTING
DOCUMENT IN THE EDITOR ➤ *p. 84*

1. Select File I Open File in Editor.
2. Browse to and open the document you want.
3. Save the new copy of the document with a different name.

CONVERT A NON-WEB DOCUMENT
TO THE HTML FORMAT ➤ *pp. 84-88*

1. Convert the document to MS Word format, RTF, or plain text.
2. Run Internet Assistant, rtf2html, or text2html on the document.
3. Open the new HTML document in Netscape Editor.

Impatient to just go ahead and make a simple home page? Jump ahead to "But Wait! I Just Want a Simple Home Page."

CAUTION

Netscape Editor has a lot of word processing features, but it's definitely not a full-fledged word processing program like Word or WordPerfect. You may want to prepare your text in whatever word processor you're comfortable with, especially while you're still settling on exact wording and having to make systematic changes.

Time to make the donuts. With Netscape, what once required two handfuls of programs and mastery of several different operating systems can now be accomplished within the warm confines of a single program. Putting aside, at least temporarily, all the issues of designing, planning, acquiring talent for, and creating an entire Web site, here's our basic approach to creating any single document.

MAKING A WEB DOCUMENT (FOR BUSY PEOPLE)

With Navigator Gold, you can create a Web document in a few simple steps:

1. Create or open the document.
2. Edit (and format) the document.
3. Save the document.
4. Publish the document.

Create or Open the Document in Netscape Editor

There are two kinds of documents you can edit in Netscape Editor—existing documents and new documents. Existing documents can be either HTML or non-Web documents.

Using Existing Documents

If you already have text or other documents that you want to include in your Web site, you can convert them to HTML and then edit them with Netscape Editor. Also, if you've created Web documents by some other means, or have some existing Web documents you'd like to work with, you can edit them in Netscape Editor as well.

habits & strategies

Also, you can use any Web document you find as a template in Netscape.

Most professional organizations maintain a backup "staging server" where they assemble an entire site (or an entire set of changes), only publishing a full set of changes when they're ready.

So there are two steps:

1. Creating or assembling text documents and,
2. Converting them to HTML.

Converting is explained in "Converting Non-Web Documents," at the end of this chapter.

It's as easy to open an existing Web document in Netscape Editor as it is to open a text document in a word processor.

Creating Documents from Scratch

Netscape provides two shortcuts to get you started with new documents. The full-service option is Netscape's Page Wizard, explained step-by-step in the next section, "But Wait! I Just Want a Simple Home Page." More varied options are available in the form of Netscape templates.

If you're feeling bold, you can start with a blank document and go from there. Type or insert text, format your document, add links and pictures, and you're done.

Edit the Document

After opening or starting a document, you'll need to fill in the text you want (or, if you're using templates, replace dummy text with real stuff). You can paste existing text from documents created in other applications, if you like. The next few chapters will fill in the details on typing, editing, formatting, hyperlinking, and more advanced design options.

Save the Document

When you're done editing the document, as with any other type of application, you'll want to save it. This is not the same thing as "publishing" the document. The difference is that saving a document means updating the local copy stored on your computer; publishing it means posting a copy of it to the Web server where it's available to the public.

Publish the Document

As mentioned in the previous section, publishing a document means transferring a copy of it to the Web server where it becomes part of a public site. In the past, this meant maintaining a separate FTP program and an FTP server with access to the Web site (or, worse yet, sending files by e-mail to a provider and waiting for them to post the changes). Now with one-button publishing, Netscape Editor can post a document (or a full set of documents) to a site.

It's a good idea to schedule a testing period after publishing the site but before *publicizing* it, so that a small group of colleagues or trusted clients can visit the site and look for errors or problems. When the testing period is concluded, you'll want to announce the page or site in the various search utilities and in other public forums on the Internet, when appropriate.

The Big Picture

We want to be careful not to blur the distinction between the fairly simple process of creating a single Web page and the more complicated endeavor of assembling and posting an entire Web site. The steps involved in putting together a site are similar to those spelled out just now but involve some overarching considerations. Instead, for an entire site, think in terms of these steps:

1. Plan the site (and think about who will maintain it and how updates will be made).
2. Assemble the documents.
3. Edit and save all the documents.
4. Publish the documents.
5. Promote the site.

BUT WAIT! I JUST WANT A SIMPLE HOME PAGE

If you are planning a more elaborate Web site, skip to the next section. If you're not sure, go back to Chapter 2 and read about the difference between a Web site and a home page.

Yes, you don't have to plan a million-dollar Web site before you can produce a simple home page. The easiest way to crank one out is with Netscape's Page Wizard. The Page Wizard is actually stored at the Netscape Web site, not on your computer, so Netscape can change it or improve it whenever they want. When you start a document based on the Page Wizard, Navigator connects you to the Page Wizard, *um,* page where you can read some instructions and then start picking and choosing elements for your page.

CAUTION

Netscape is changing and improving their templates and Page Wizard all the time, so the illustrations shown here and the step-by-step instructions may no longer precisely match what you'll see online, but the gist of it should remain the same.

Make sure you're connected to the Net before choosing From Wizard from the submenu, because Navigator will attempt to connect to the Netscape Page Wizard page.

When you've finished filling out the Page Wizard form, the wizard makes your page for you, suitable for downloading.

The following are instructions for using the Page Wizard, as of the date of publication of this book:

1. To begin, select File I New Document I From Wizard. This connects you to the Netscape Page Wizard page, which is divided into three frames, two of which are, at first, blank (see Figure 4.1).
2. Read the brief introduction in the non-blank, working frame, scrolling to see the entire text.
3. When you're ready, click the Start button. Instructions will appear in the upper-left frame while the upper-right frame turns into a Preview area for the page you'll create (See Figure 4.2).
4. Read the simple instructions that appear in the upper-left frame.

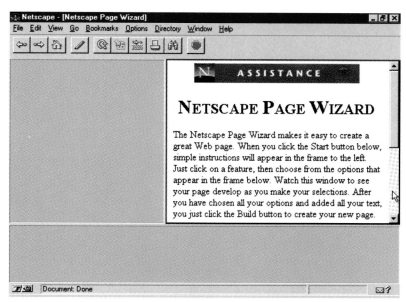

Figure 4.1 Read the brief introduction in the upper-right frame and then click the Start button

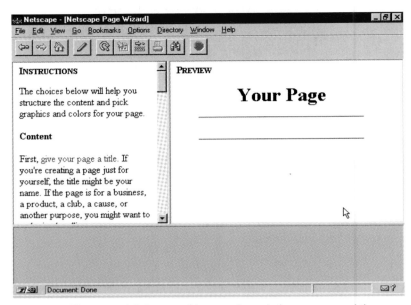

Figure 4.2 The upper-left frame guides you through the process and the upper-right frame shows you what you're doing

Adding Content to Your Page

First, the Wizard prompts you to supply the content for your page.

1. Click **give your page a title**.
   A box appears in the bottom frame.

2. Type a title in the box (replacing the dummy title text).
3. Click the Apply button.
   Your title appears in the Preview area.
4. Click **type an introduction** in the upper-left frame.
   A slightly larger box appears in the bottom frame.
5. Type something about yourself or your organization in the box.
6. Click Apply.

habits & strategies

If you're reading through these steps before actually trying this, think about getting the Web addresses together before you start. That will make it easier to type them (or, better yet, copy and paste them into the document).

You will make all your choices in the bottom frame.

CAUTION

If you are confused by the topic of hotlinks (hyperlinks) and unsure of how to enter URLs, you can skip the next five steps (for now).

The introduction you typed appears on the Preview of your page.

7. Click **add some hotlinks to other Web pages**.
8. Type the name of one of your favorite Web pages in the Name box.
9. Type that page's URL (Web address) in the URL box.
10. Click Apply.
11. Repeat as often as you wish (see Figure 4.3).

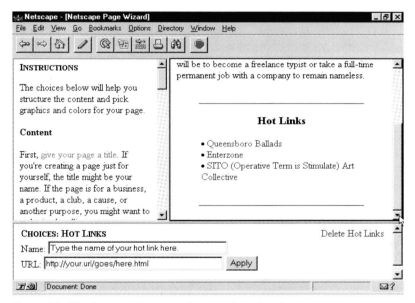

Figure 4.3 Here's your chance to plug your favorite sites

12. Click **type a paragraph of text to serve as a conclusion** in the upper-left frame.

    A box appears in the bottom frame.

13. Type a little more about yourself or your organization in the box.
14. Click Apply.

The conclusion appears on the Preview of your page (see Figure 4.4).

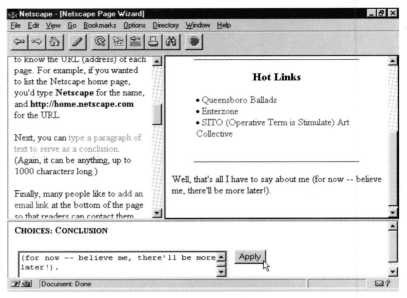

Figure 4.4   Your page is starting to take shape (albeit in a slightly more crunched form than it will have later, when it can fill the entire browser screen)

If you change your mind about the links, you can click Delete Hot Links *in the bottom frame to eliminate the links you've added and start over.*

If you want people to be able to reach you by e-mail through your page, follow the next few steps:

1. Click **add an email link**.
2. Type your e-mail address in the box that appears.
3. Click Apply.

Now the content of your document is complete and you can spruce up its appearance.

Designing and Formatting Your Page

Page Wizard helps you choose color combinations, background patterns, and fancy line and bullet styles for your page.

1. Scroll down to the Looks section of the Instructions in the upper-left frame and read the brief introduction.
2. To choose one of the Wizard's pre-designed color combinations, click **preset color combination**.
3. Choose one of the color combinations that appear in the bottom frame.

CHOICES: COLOR COMBINATION

Your page appears in the Preview with the colors you selected (see Figure 4.5).

If none of those combinations appeal to you, you can select each element separately. (Skip the next few steps if you like the preset colors just fine.)

1. Click **background color**.
2. Choose a background color.

CHOICES: BACKGROUND COLOR

3. Click **background pattern**.
4. Choose a background pattern.

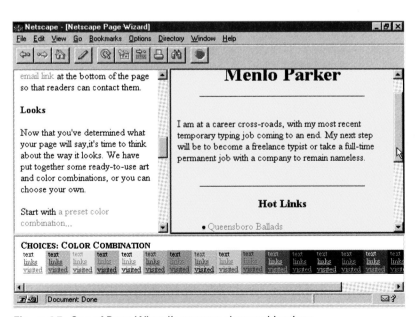

Figure 4.5 One of Page Wizard's preset color combinations

CAUTION

Make sure you don't choose such a dazzling pattern that the text on your page ends up illegible.

Figure 4.6 shows the Preview with a background pattern.

5. Click **text color**.
6. Choose a text color.
7. Click **link color**.
8. Choose a link color.

CHOICES: LINK COLOR

9. Click **visited link color**.
10. Choose a color for links, once they've been clicked.

Finally, you can select a bullet and horizontal rule style, to add a little panache to your page (very little).

1. Click **choose a bullet style**.
2. Select one of the graphical bullet elements offered (notice that a few of them are animated).

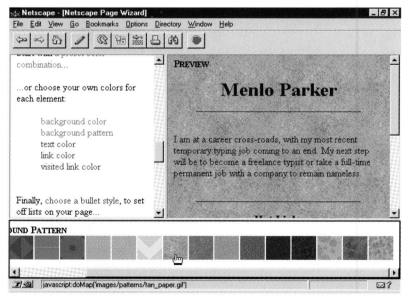

Figure 4.6 Background patterns are very popular on the Web. The small swatches "tile" to create a seamless pattern

CHOICES: BULLET STYLE

3. Click **choose a horizontal rule style**.
4. Select one of the graphical lines (you can scroll or increase the size of the frame, as shown in Figure 4.7, to see all of the rules).

habits & strategies

If there's something you don't like about the way the page came out, press the Back button to return to the Page Wizard, redesign the page, and click the Build button again.

For an alternative to Netscape's Page Wizard, you can download a stand-alone wizard program from the Net, such as Web Wizard **(http://www.halcyon.com/ artamedia/webwizard/).** *(A Mac version should be available soon.) CompuServe offers a wizard to help members set up home pages at the Our World site* **(http://ourworld.compuserve.com)**

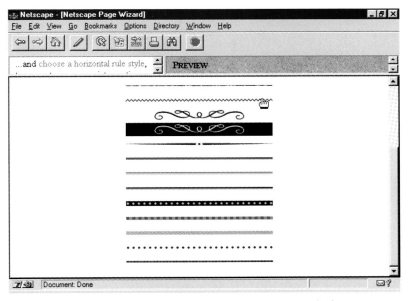

Figure 4.7 Choose a horizontal rule style to finish your page design

Finish the Page

If you change your mind about any of your decisions, just click again on the choices in the instructions frame and make different selections until you're satisfied. When you are, you can finish the page.

1. Scroll down the upper-left frame and read the rest of the instructions.
2. Click the Build button.

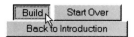

Your page is assembled (with a free plug for Netscape at the bottom), ready for you to save to your own computer. From this point on, the procedure is the same as for saving any document from the Web to your local computer for editing with Netscape Editor. Here's what you do:

3. To save the page to your computer, click the Edit button. This brings up the Save Remote Document dialog box (see Figure 4.8).

4. Click the Save button.
   Netscape will warn you against stealing other people's artwork. (Good advice! Use art you either own or have permission for!)

5. Click OK.
   The Save As dialog box will appear.

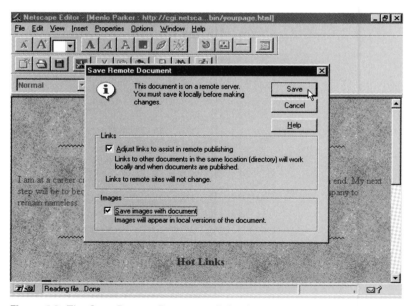

Figure 4.8 The Save Remote Document dialog box makes sure you get all the pieces of the page you want with all the references correct

6. Select a folder in which to save this document (and maybe your entire site).
7. Type a file name for the document.
8. Click OK.

To publish your new page to a public Web site, see Chapter 13.

STARTING A WEB DOCUMENT WITH A TEMPLATE

Netscape also provides some document templates for specific purposes. These contain recommended layout and structure as well as boilerplate text you can replace with your own specifics. This is a great way to get your documents started, and worry about editing them into shape later.

trends

You can expect that Netscape as well as independent developers and volunteers from the Net community will start creating and posting more templates that you can download and reuse from the Internet. A lot of service providers are starting to offer templates to their subscribers, for example.

Because of Netscape's simple one-button Edit command, you can also take, as a model, any Web document out there that you like, copy it to your hard disk, and work from it as a template. Just be sure you're not infringing on anyone's copyrights! (It's best to communicate with anyone whose work you're drawing on heavily.)

Let's cover the bona fide templates first.

Starting a Web Document with a Netscape Template

To start a Web document using a Netscape template, first select File I New Document I From Template.

CAUTION

Make sure you're connected to the Net before choosing this option, because Navigator will attempt to connect to the Netscape Templates page.

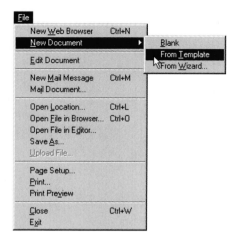

The steps mention that you should link to any companies you name "as a courtesy." Naturally, you'll want to link to any company or entity that you're affiliated with or that you support, but you're under no obligation to include a link (basically, an advertisement) for any company you mention.

This connects you to the Netscape Web Page Templates page. Read the couple of screenfuls of introductory material at the top of the page. Then read the overview of steps for using a template.

Choose a Template

The options include Netscape's Page Wizard (covered in the previous section), and a number of categories, including:

- Personal/Family
- Company/Small Business
- Department
- Product/Service
- Special Interest Group *and*
- Interesting and Fun

But read each item separately, since some of them don't fit too well in their categories. (For example, we'd put Home Sale Announcement under Personal/Family instead of Company/Small Business.)

Select and click a Template name. Navigator will take you to the template (see Figure 4.9).

Click the Edit button on the toolbar. Navigator will display the Save Remote Document dialog box (see Figure 4.8). Click Save. Netscape will warn you against stealing other people's artwork. (This is indeed good advice. Only use art you either own or have permission for!) Click OK. The Save As dialog box will appear. Select a folder in which to save

To build an entire site on your computer before publishing it to the Net, choose or create an empty directory in which to keep all its documents together in the exact relationship they'll share when published. You may also want to call the root home page "index.html."

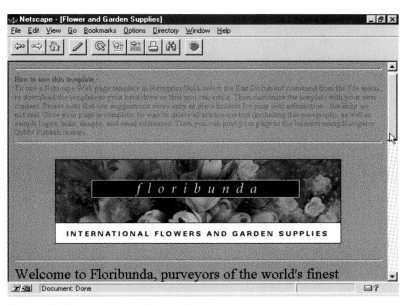

Figure 4.9 The Flower and Garden Supplies template, the closest we could find for our fictional travel agency/guided tour company

this document (and maybe your entire site). Type a file name for the document, and click OK.

Edit and Clean Up the Document

Edit and customize the template to suit your needs. For example, start by removing the warning (but read it first!). Click and drag to select the horizontal rule at the top of the page and the text beneath it, as you would select text and graphics in a word processor.

> **How to use this template**
> To use a Netscape Web page template in Navigator Gold, select the Edit Document command from the File menu to download the template to your hard drive so that you can edit it. Then customize the template with your own content. Please note that our suggestions serve only as place holders for your own information - the links are not real. Once your page is complete, be sure to delete all extraneous text (including this paragraph), as well as sample logos, links, images, and email addresses. Then you can post your page to the Internet using Navigator Gold's Publish feature.

Then press DELETE. Voilá! The line and text disappear. If you change your mind, select Edit I Undo or press CTRL-Z to undo your most recent action. For more on typing, editing, and formatting text, see

habits & strategies

If you plan to make several documents based on this one, save it as a template (with a generic name) and then open it and save it under a new name each time for each new document based on it. Opening existing documents is covered in the section "Opening an Existing Local Document," coming up.

Chapter 5. Rewrite and hack that document into shape. Paste in text from other documents if you need to.

Leave the dummy template art in the document at first, as "place holders," so you can replace them with your own art later without having to set things like the alignment options yourself.

When you're ready to publish your new page to a public Web site, see Chapter 13.

Using Any Web Document as a Template

We first learned HTML by using the browser's View Source command to see the code underlying the pages we liked. Now, "borrowing" other people's design ideas is even easier, since all you have to do is download a copy of what you're viewing, save it, and start modifying it.

Say you wanted to base your home page on the Whirled-Wide Med home page (at **http://syx.com/x/busy/wwm.html**). You could point Navigator Gold at that address and get the page on your screen (see Figure 4.10).

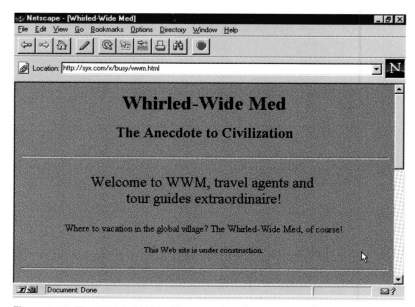

Figure 4.10 The Whirled-Wide Med travel and tour agency home page

Now, to start working on your own copy of this page, just click the Edit button. Navigator will display the Save Remote Document dialog box (see Figure 4.8). Click Save. Netscape will warn you against stealing other people's artwork. (Truly good advice indeed! Use art you either own or have permission for!) Click OK. The Save As dialog box will appear. Select a folder to save this document (and maybe your entire site) in. Type a file name for the document, and click OK.

Does this sound familiar? It's the exact same process used to download "real" templates from the Netscape site. From this point, follow the same advice we gave you in the previous section!

STARTING WITH A BLANK SLATE

It *is* possible to face up to that proverbial blank white page and just write your own Web document without cribbing other people's ideas or boilerplate. To do so, select File | New Document | Blank.

Netscape Editor will create a new document named Untitled and let you go at it (see Figure 4.11).

CAUTION

Naturally, if you are creating a commercial Web site, you should not appropriate anyone else's text, art, or ideas without their consent.

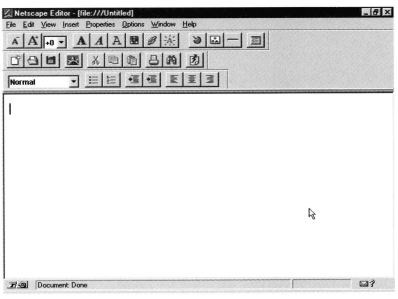

Figure 4.11 A new blank Web document ready for you to start typing

Jump ahead to Chapter 5 to start typing, editing, and formatting your document.

OPENING AN EXISTING LOCAL DOCUMENT

If you have a document you've already started working on (even one you've created in another Web editor or a plain-text editor), you can open it in Netscape Editor and handle it the way you do your new pages.

To open an existing Web document, select File | Open File in Editor (from the browser window) or just File | Open File (from the editor window).

This brings up the Open dialog box.

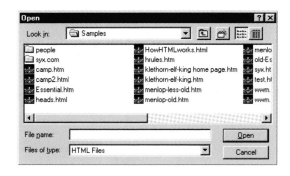

Browse to and open the document you want. It will appear in the editor window (see Figure 4.12).

Be sure to save any new copy of a document (after you've opened it in Netscape Editor) with a different name to make sure you don't lose your original version of the document, in case something doesn't come out the way you want.

CONVERTING NON-WEB DOCUMENTS

Often when you start building a Web site, you already have existing documents (or images) that you plan to adapt to the Web. If the documents are already designed and formatted (as opposed to memos and draft text), then you'll want to preserve as much of the formatting as possible, so you don't have to repeat that step. Fortu-

CAUTION

If you've used any kind of HTML coding that Netscape Editor doesn't understand, the program will mark that formatting as unrecognized HTML tags (or, in some cases, convert the tags to something similar, possibly producing results you don't want.

habits & strategies

Remember, if you're going to try "staging" your Web site in one location before publishing it en masse to the Web, then your local computer is the perfect staging ground. It's easy to open files directly off your own computer rather than constantly downloading them from a remote Web site.

See Chapter 7 for more on inserting hyperlinks.

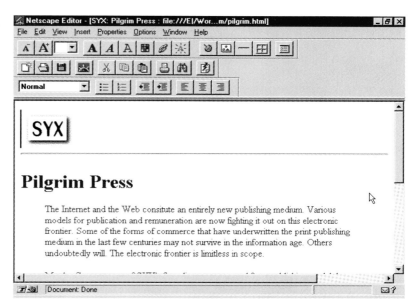

Figure 4.12 A document Christian created before getting Navigator Gold, opened for editing in Netscape Editor

nately, the formatting HTML tags correspond to a fairly standard set of formatting features that most programs can handle. (In fact, word processing and desktop publishing programs usually have more text formatting features than the Web does.)

This means that you can often convert the existing documents into, at least partially, formatted Web documents. You'll still need to insert the hyperlinks yourself. Also, no conversion tools or programs work perfectly, so you may end up having to reproduce some of the formatting in Netscape Editor.

For that matter, not all document formats can easily be converted. You may need to convert documents into some interim format, something more universally readable, such as Word for Windows 2.0 format or RTF (rich text format), and then into HTML. As a final resort, you can always convert written documents to "plain text" format (usually with the extension .txt). You will lose all of the formatting, but at least you won't have to retype the text. (Most programs that handle documents have a "save as text" option, often on a list in the Save As dialog box.)

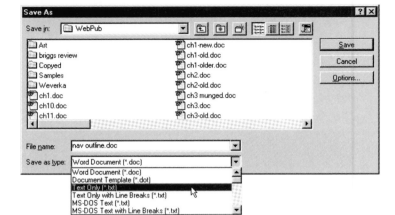

See Chapter 8 for more on converting existing image files.

Finding Converters

Depending on the file formats you're starting with and the type of computers you use, you'll need to explore different conversion options. For example, even Macintosh, UNIX, and other users averse to Microsoft's dominant position in the computer world can recognize that the Word for Windows document format is very widely understood by competing programs, even on other platforms. In that capacity, it functions as a lingua franca.

If you can get a document into Word format on a Windows computer, and you have Word for Windows, then you can convert your documents to HTML with the Internet Assistant add-in for Word for Windows. Download Internet Assistant (for free) from the Microsoft Web site (**http://www.microsoft.com**) in the Products section, under Microsoft Office and Word for Windows. (WordPerfect devotees should download the analogous Internet Publisher add-in for WordPerfect from **http://www.wordperfect.com**.)

bookmark

*Download Internet Assistant from the Microsoft Web site (**http://www.microsoft.com**). Download Internet Publisher from the WordPerfect Web site (**http://www.wordperfect.com**).*

If you can get your documents into RTF (rich text format), then there are two ways you can convert them to HTML. One is to open them in a word processor that can save in HTML format (such as Word with Internet Assistant installed or, yes, WordPerfect with Internet Publisher installed). The other is to convert them directly with an RTF-to-HTML conversion utility. There are different programs for different types of computers (often with similar sounding names—for example, there's RTFtoHTML for the Macintosh, rtftohtml for UNIX, and rtf2html for Windows).

The best resources we know for converters are the W3 Organization's page (**http://www.w3.org/hypertext/WWW/Tools/Filters.html**) and the Web Designer's page of HTML Converters and Templates (**http://limestone.kosone.com/people/nelsonl/convert.htm**).

---

bookmark

The W3 converter page is at **http://www.w3.org/hypertext/WWW/Tools/Filters.html**. *The Web Designer's HTML Converters page is at* **http://limestone.kosone.com/people/nelsonl/convert.htm**.

Depending on the program you download, you either run it at a command line, specifying the name of the file you want to convert, drop the document onto the program's icon (as with the RTFtoHTML Macintosh program), or install the filter into a word processing program and use it to save RTF documents in HTML format.

Converting with Internet Assistant

Internet Assistant gives Word the ability to save any document in HTML format (among other things). Also, since you can open an RTF document in Word, you can use it to convert RTF documents to HTML. So all you do is open your Word or RTF document and then select File | Save As. Give the document a new name and select HTML Document in the Save As drop-down list box.

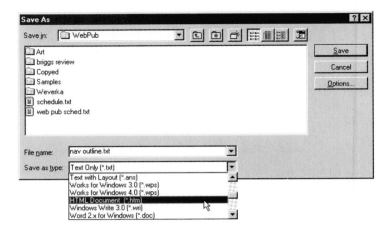

Then click OK. After that, just open the document in Netscape Editor and start formatting it (as described in Chapter 5).

Converting Plain Text Files

To prepare a plain text file, first copy it and give the new document a file name with an .html (or .htm) extension. Then open the document in Netscape Editor and start editing it, as we'll explain in Chapter 5.

WHAT'S NEXT?

Once you've started a new page, you have to fill it with information, format it, and link it to other pages. The next few chapters will help you do just that.

Typing, Editing, and Formatting Text

91

Up here in North America it can get pretty cold!
summer, without cold 'n' wet weather gear. (See

Here we've picked four of our favorite spots to la
realize that we haven't put the fly on yet.

FAST FORWARD

TYPE TEXT IN A WEB DOCUMENT ➤ *p. 96*

- Just type.
- Let Netscape handle word-wrapping.
- Press ENTER to start a new paragraph.

TITLE A WEB DOCUMENT ➤ *p. 97*

1. Select Properties I Document.
2. Type a title in the Title box.
3. Click OK.

SAVE A WEB DOCUMENT ➤ *pp. 97-98*

Press the Save button.

of our favorite spots to

EDIT A WEB DOCUMENT ➤ *p. 98*

First, select the text you want to affect and then

- Delete the selection,
- Cut the selection,
- Copy the selection, *and/or*
- Paste the selection.

STRUCTURE YOUR DOCUMENT ➤ *pp. 99-102*

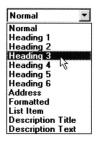

- Select heading levels from the Paragraph style drop-down list.
- Insert breaks with SHIFT-ENTER.
- Insert horizontal rules by clicking the Insert Horizontal Rules button.

FORMAT YOUR DOCUMENT ➤ *pp. 102-110*

Make a selection and then

- Click the Bold, Italic, or Fixed Width buttons,
- Click the Indent or Unindent buttons,
- Click the Left Alignment, Center, or Right Alignment buttons, *or*
- Pull-down the Paragraph style list-box and select Address.

PREVIEW YOUR DOCUMENT
IN THE BROWSER WINDOW ➤ *p. 110*

1. Save the document.
2. Click the View in Browser button.

If you've ever used a word processor or even a text editor, then Netscape Editor should be very easy for you to learn. It has fewer features than most word processors because HTML documents don't have many of the elements of paper documents, such as page numbers. (It would be nice if the makers of Netscape Editor added a Search and Replace feature, though!)

habits & strategies

You can also right-click in different places on the screen (if you have a Mac, click and hold down the mouse button) to pop-up a "context-sensitive" menu. (And that just means a menu of likely commands you might want to use in that location.)

trends

Feature by feature, Netscape will keep adding to its Editor module until it's virtually a full-fledged word processor. (Word processing programs, such as Word for Windows, are also busily turning themselves into full-fledged Web-document editors.)

The idea is about the same: you see what you're typing in the main window and you give commands by choosing them from menus or by clicking shortcut buttons.

NETSCAPE EDITOR TOOLBARS

Most of the useful editing and formatting commands are available on the three toolbars at the top of the window, the Character Properties toolbar,

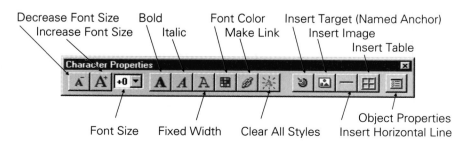

If you've got an 800 x 600 screen, you might want to plop the Character Properties toolbar to the right of the File/Edit Tools toolbar to increase the amount of real estate in the main window.

Also, in Windows, if you position the mouse pointer over a button without clicking, a little yellow label will appear on the screen, telling you the name of the button.

the File/Edit Tools toolbar,

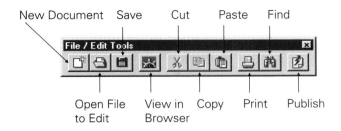

and the Paragraph Properties toolbar.

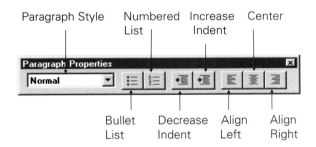

You can tell what most of the buttons do by their names.

On the Character Properties toolbar, the Fixed Width button applies TT (typewriter) formatting to selected text. The Object Properties button lets you set whatever options are available for any selection.

On the File/Edit Tools toolbar, the View in Browser button opens a new browser window and opens the document you're working on (so you can, for example, test the links). The Publish button sends your document and related files to your Web server.

On the Paragraph Properties toolbar, the Decrease Indent and Increase Indent buttons use the UL (unordered list) formatting to force indentation. Although you can't be sure that all browsers will interpret the beginning of a list as an indent, as my technical editor pointed out, most browsers will in fact interpret the logical unordered-list tag as a physical indentation.

TYPING YOUR DOCUMENT

To begin with, just start typing as you would in a word processing document. Netscape Editor handles word-wrapping for you. To start a new paragraph, press ENTER (see Figure 5.1).

You can move your insertion point the usual ways, either by pressing an arrow key or by clicking your mouse where you want the insertion point to appear. As your document gets longer, you can use the scroll bars to move around in it.

SAVE REGULARLY!

As soon as you've typed anything of consequence at all, save your document. Save it just about every time you change it. Netscape Editor has no "autosave" feature, so you're on your own as far as saving documents goes. Saving is more important than flossing! Think back to the last time you lost *a lot* of work by not saving. Don't let it happen again.

CAUTION

It's too bad, but currently Netscape has no way of assigning a new default folder to save in, so you have to change the directory you're looking at every time you start Netscape Editor. Be careful not to save a new file in the Netscape program folder by mistake!

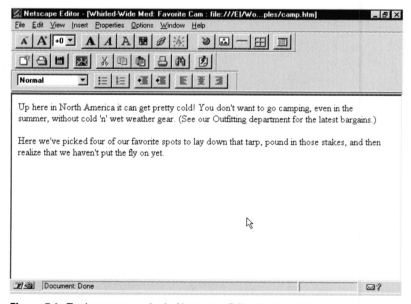

Figure 5.1 Typing paragraphs in Netscape Editor is about the same as typing them in any modern word processing program

habits & strategies

If your Web page is added to someone's bookmark list or to another Web page, the title will most likely be associated with the link. Choose titles wisely. For example, we used to call Enterzone's home page "Enterzone Home Page," until we saw it appearing that way on other people's pages and changed it to just "Enterzone."

Giving Your Document a Title

Unless you plan to keep the name of the document you stole, *er,* borrowed—"Floribunda Flower Supplies," or whatever the title was— you should give your document a new, real title before you save it for the first time. Once you've done that, you can forget about your title.

To give your document a title, select Properties | Document to bring up the Document Properties dialog box (see Figure 5.2).

Type a new title in the title box and then click OK. Netscape Editor will display as much of the new title as possible in the title bar, along with the name of the source file (which, since you haven't saved it yet, is still file:///Untitled in Netscape's parlance).

> Netscape Editor - [Whirled-Wide Med: Favorite Cam : file:///Untitled]

Saving for the First Time and Thereafter

The first time you save your document, you have to give it a name. Keep it simple. It's best to plan out ahead of time what the names of the various files are going to be.

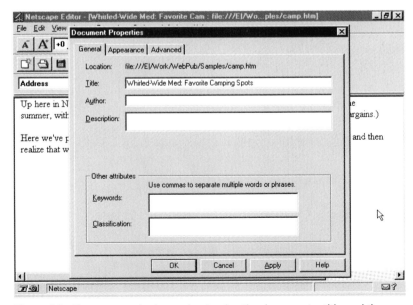

Figure 5.2 For now, you're just going to give the document a title and then close this dialog box. (Later, you'll do more with it)

Remember, you can undo

multiple actions by pressing

CTRL-Z *(*COMMAND-Z *on the Mac)*

or slecting Edit |Undo repeatedly.

You can paste text or images

directly from other programs.

Select text in WordPerfect, say,

and copy it. Then switch back to

Netscape and paste the selection

there. So far, you can't drag text

selections and drop them, but an

upcoming version of Navigator

Gold may include that feature also.

The home page of a complicated set of pages is often called index.html because most Web servers use index.html as their default file name. This can save your readers some typing when they visit— it's easier to type **http://foo.com** than **http://foo.com/company_ home_page.html**. Unless you specify something else, Netscape assumes you want to go to **http://** something and guesses **.com** if you leave that out too, and since Web servers can be set to recognize more than one version of an address, your site can be as easy to reach as **syx** or as hard as **http:// www.syx.com/index.html**.

To save and name your document, click the Save button. Choose the folder you want to save your page in. Then type a file name and click Save.

After you've saved the document once, you can just click the Save button to save additional changes as you go. Remember, saving is not the same as publishing. Saving updates the local copy on your computer. Publishing updates the Web server.

EDITING YOUR DOCUMENT

As you type or revise a document, you inevitably find mistakes, make corrections, change things, and so on. Yes, you do these things in Netscape Editor much the same way you would in a word processor. You can select text by clicking and dragging. (You can select horizontal rules and images just as easily.) To delete selections, just press the DELETE key. To cut a selection so you can move it elsewhere, click the Cut button (or right-click and select Cut).

To copy a selection instead of moving it, click the Copy button (or right-click I Copy), move the insertion point where you want to copy the selection and then click the Paste button (or right-click I Paste).

FORMATTING FOR STRUCTURE

OK. The boring preliminaries are out of the way. You can start formatting your Web document! Remember, attention spans on the Web are short and people are constantly jumping away to other spots. The last thing people want to see is a dense screenful of gray-looking text. Use headings to grab attention and clearly mark the different parts of your document. Insert line breaks and horizontal rules to space out the text, keep it organized, and make it easy to read.

Making Headings

It's easy to make headings with the Paragraph Style drop-down list box on the Paragraph Properties toolbar.

If you want to have a contact address at the foot of your document, see the "Contact Addresses" section later in this chapter.

Headings appear left-aligned by default but can also be centered or right-aligned. See "Paragraph Formatting," later in this chapter.

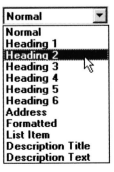

Just select the text you want to make into a heading (or put the insertion point where you want to start typing your new heading), click in the Paragraph Style list, and select the heading level you want. After you type the heading and press ENTER, the next line will be a regular paragraph (see Figure 5.3).

Line Breaks

Remember, you're making a new paragraph every time you press ENTER. If you want to start a new line but stay in the same paragraph (in most browsers, this prevents skipping a line), you can just press SHIFT-ENTER. This inserts a line break, and is commonly referred to as "breaking" the line of text. A line break is not the beginning of a new paragraph.

You can also prevent a line from breaking in any specific space (at least for Netscape browsers), by inserting a non-breaking space, as it's called. Just select the existing space (or position the insertion point where you want the no-break-space to appear), and then press SHIFT-SPACE BAR. You won't see anything different (unless you looked at the source document, in which case you'd see).

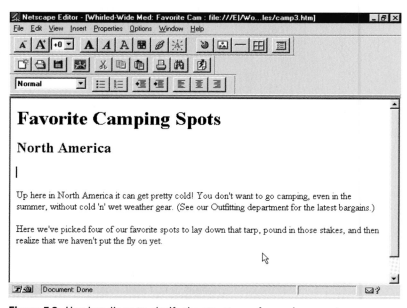

Figure 5.3 Use headings to clarify the structure of your documents

Horizontal Rules (Lines)

Another way to structure a document is to insert horizontal lines (rules) to separate different sections. To insert a rule at any time, just click the Insert Horizontal Rule button.

Figure 5.4 shows a horizontal rule. It separates an introductory section and list of contents from the first item on a page.

You can also customize the thickness, width, and appearance of horizontal rules. To do so, select a rule (click anywhere on it) and then select Properties | Horizontal Line (or just right-click on the rule—click and hold with a Macintosh—and then choose Horizontal line properties from the menu that pops up). This brings up the Horizontal Line Properties dialog box.

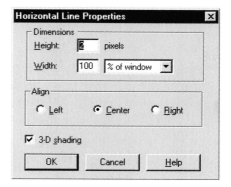

- To change the thickness of the line from the default of 2 pixels, type a different number of pixels in the Height box.
- To change the width of the line from the default of 100% of the screen width, first choose either *% of window* or *pixels* and then type a percentage or number of pixels for the width of the line.
- To change the alignment of the line, choose Left, Center, or Right.
- To eliminate the 3-D "beveled" appearance of the line, uncheck 3-D shading.

To mark text as "preformatted" (what Netscape calls Formatted), select it, and then choose Formatted on the Paragraph style drop-down list. You'll probably then have to reinsert the necessary line breaks (!).

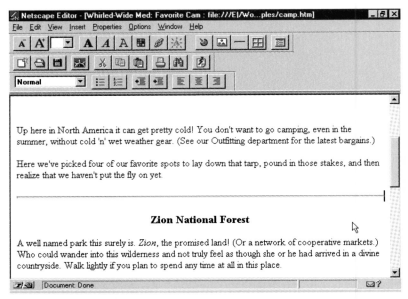

Figure 5.4 The first destination featured on WWM's Favorite Camping Spots page for North America

Navigator does not do underlining. If you need to use an HTML tag Netscape doesn't offer, you can type in the tag yourself. See Chapter 11 for more on inserting custom tags.

FORMATTING FOR DESIGN AND CLARITY

Netscape Editor makes it very easy to format characters and align text in different ways. It's usually just a matter of selecting text and then clicking a button, choosing an item from a drop-down list or menu, or—at its most complicated—selecting an item from a dialog box.

Character Formatting

Technically, HTML allows for two types of character formatting, called logical and physical tags. Logical tags, such as those for emphasis or to indicate that text is someone's name or a cited title of some work, are not supported by Netscape Editor (except for Address formatting).

Instead, Netscape Editor provides commands for physical formatting, which tells browsers literally how to display the text. For example, most browsers interpret the logical tag for emphasis coding as italics, but not all do. However, if you mark text with the physical tag for italics formatting, all browsers that can display italics will display your text with them (some, like plain text browsers, can't display italics).

Bold, Italics, and Fixed Width

The most popular forms of character formatting—bold, italic, and "fixed width"—are available from the toolbars.

To make existing text bold, for example, select the text and then click the Bold button. To type new boldface text, position the insertion point, click the Bold button, and then start typing. The button will appear "pushed in."

When you want to continue typing in regular (unbold) text, click the button again and keep going.

Superscript, Subscript, Strikethrough, and Blink

For the occasionally useful types of character formatting offered by Netscape Editor, just select the text you want to format and choose Properties I Character. Then select the type of formatting you want from the submenu that appears:

CAUTION

You may have trouble communicating with old-time users of HTML if you use Netscape's terminology when discussing Formatted text. Everyone else who works with Web documents calls such text "preformatted" text, because it keeps whatever formatting, such as line breaks, tabs, and extra spaces, instead of getting "normal" HTML formatting.

103

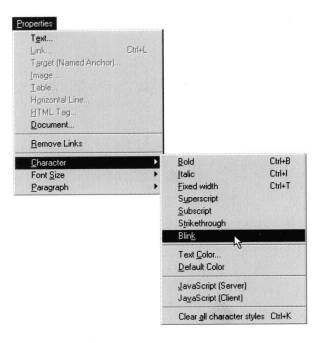

For the record,

- Superscript places text above the baseline and reduces its size (as in "e=mc^2").
- Subscript places text below the baseline and reduces its size (as in "H_2O").
- Strikethrough (used most often to indicate deleted text) marks text with a horizontal line (as in "The offer is $100,~~000~~.00").
- Blink makes text blink on and off.

Font Size

There are two easy ways to change the size of text. Either way, select the text first (or place the insertion point where you intend to type the unusual-sized text).

- To reduce the selected text in size by one unit, click the Decrease Font Size button.
- To increase the selected text in size by one unit, click the Increase Font Size button.

CAUTION

The blink formatting tag was introduced by Netscape and is widely held in disrepute. Aside from the occasional humorous or very subtle use of blink, it rarely fails to bring disfavor onto a page it adorns.

*If you intend to change the font
size of headings, apply the
heading format first, which will
cause an automatic change in
size. Then manually adjust the
size further.*

- To select an exact amount of increase or decrease, click the Font Size drop-down list and choose from the range of seven font sizes.

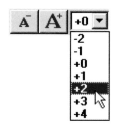

Font Color

You can change the color of any selected text (or text you're about to type) by clicking the Font Color button.

It brings up the Color dialog box.

*See Chapter 8 for how to set up a
default color scheme for the text,
background, and links, before and after
they're clicked.*

Choose a color from the Basic Colors list and then click OK. Figure 5.5 shows a document with adjusted-size fonts and colored headings.

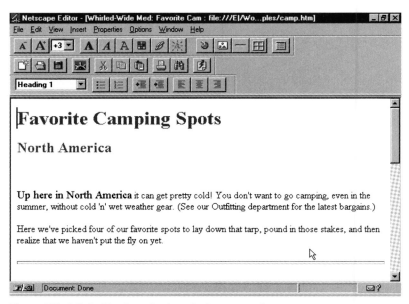

Figure 5.5 A little bit of a color in a design goes a long way

One-Stop Character Formatting

If you want to apply more than one type of formatting to a selection, right-click (click and hold with a Mac) and choose Character Properties (or select Properties I Text and choose the Character tab).

This brings up the Properties dialog box with its Character tab selected (see Figure 5.6).

Choose a color, if you like. In fact, select as many forms of character formatting as you feel like piling up on your selection. (You can, for example, combine bold and italics.) Change the size if it suits you. When you are done, click OK.

Removing Character Formatting

If you change your mind about some character formatting you've applied, select the text again and then click the Clear All Styles button.

Paragraph Formatting

There are a few formatting effects you can apply to entire paragraphs (as well as to headings and other kinds of text). Among them are indentation, alignment, blockquotes, and addresses.

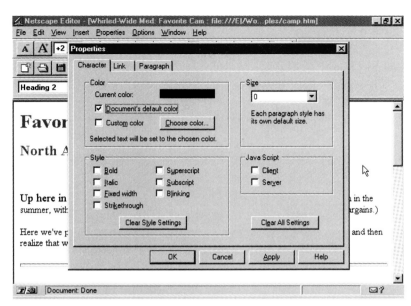

Figure 5.6 The Character tab of the Properties dialog box

If you are working with a list (see Chapter 6), then the indentation buttons create legitimate HTML sublists.

Physical Indentation

One type of paragraph formatting is indentation, which, as we mentioned before, is not true indentation but rather a trick using the way most lists are displayed. To use this effect, select the text you want to indent (or unindent), or position the insertion point at the new indented (or unindented) paragraph you want to type, and then click one of the indentation buttons.

Left, Center, and Right Alignment

More useful are the alignment commands. Technically, they're a mishmash: Left Alignment just restores the default (no alignment) status of a paragraph; Center applies the Netscape-only CENTER tag (but it's very widely accepted); and Right Alignment uses an HTML 3.2 tag that may not work for some browsers yet. As with all the other shortcut buttons, first select the text you want to affect and then click a button.

Block Quotations

If you are quoting more than a couple of lines of some source document, it's customary to set the quotation off from the main text in its own paragraph, typically indented from either margin. To apply this kind of formatting, right-click (click and hold with a Mac) on a selected quotation and choose Paragraph Formatting from the menu that pops up (or select Properties I Text and choose the Paragraph tab).

This brings up the Properties dialog box with the Paragraph tab selected (see Figure 5.7).

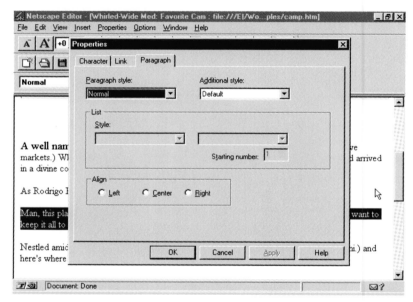

Figure 5.7 The Paragraph tab of the Properties dialog box

Click the Additional Style drop-down list and choose Block Quote.

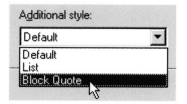

Then click OK. Figure 5.8 shows a block quotation set off from a main paragraph. (The italics were added separately.)

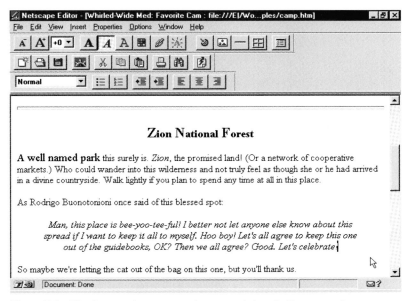

Figure 5.8   Block quotations are easier to read than in-line quotations

Contact Addresses

If you want to mark an e-mail address or the creator's name as an address, just select it, pull down the Paragraph styles drop-down list box and choose Address.

See Chapter 7 to learn how to make your e-mail address a live link to your mail box.

If you're creating a footer, insert a horizontal rule, type the date and your name, and then type your e-mail address.

Last updated March 29, 1996 / Menlo Parker / menlop@syx.com

You can save a document with this footer and reuse it in the future as a template (see "Creating a Master Document" later in this chapter).

PREVIEWING YOUR DOCUMENT

When you want to see how your current document will look in the Netscape browser window, save it. Then click the View in Browser button.

Netscape will open a new browser window and open your current document in it (see Figure 5.9).

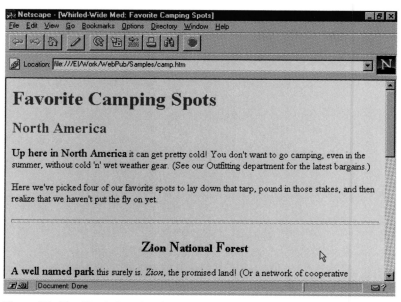

Figure 5.9 The North America Camping Spots page in browser view

It's possible to designate a local document as your preferred document template. Select Options Editor Preferences, click the General tab, and in the Location box in the New document template area, type file:/// (yes, three forward slashes) followed by the path and file name of the document you want to use (separate each folder level with a /).

CREATING A MASTER DOCUMENT

If you plan to base an entire Web site or even a section of a site (such as a catalog) on a basic document design, create a formatted document with minimal dummy text, save it, and then reuse it as a template. When you want to base a new document on the template, open it and immediately save a copy of it under a new name (using File Save As).

WHAT'S NEXT?

In the next chapter we'll show you how to create various kinds of lists, including numbered lists, bulleted lists, and definition lists. In Chapter 7 you'll learn how to link your documents together and Chapter 8 will show you how use graphics to illustrate your pages.

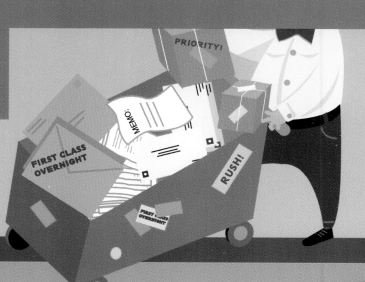

Making Lists

FAST FORWARD

**MAKE A NUMBERED OR BULLETED
LIST FROM SCRATCH** ➤ *pp. 117-119*

1. Click the Bullet List or Numbered List button.
2. Start typing the list and press ENTER after each list entry.
3. Click the Bullet List or Numbered List button again when
   you're done.

**CONVERT PARAGRAPHS YOU'VE ENTERED INTO
A BULLETED OR NUMBERED LIST** ➤ *pp. 117-119*

1. Select the paragraphs.
2. Click the Bullet List or Numbered List button.

CREATE A DEFINITION LIST ➤ *pp. 119-121*

1. Either place the cursor where you want to type the definition
   term or select the term if you've already typed it.
2. Pull down the Paragraph style drop-down list and choose
   Description Title.
3. Either place the cursor where you want to type the definition
   or select the definition if you've already typed it.
4. Pull down the Paragraph style drop-down list and choose
   Description Text.

INCLUDE A LIST WITHIN A LIST ➤ *pp. 123-124*

1. Place the cursor where you want the subordinate list to start.
2. Press the Increase Indent button to continue with the same
   kind of list, or press the Bullet List or Numbered List button
   to make the subordinate list different from the main list.

CHANGE THE BULLET TYPE OR
NUMBERING SCHEME OF A LIST ➤ *pp. 124-125*

1. Select the list and open the Properties dialog box (right-click and select List Properties).
2. To change the bullet style, choose Unnumbered list from the List area's Style drop-down list, and then choose Automatic, Solid circle, Solid square, or Open square in the Bullet style drop-down list.
3. To change the numbering scheme, choose Numbered List in the List area's Style drop-down list, and then choose Automatic; 1,2,3...; I,II,III...; A,B,C...; or a,b,c... in the Number style drop-down list.

START NUMBERING A LIST WITH A
NUMBER OTHER THAN 1 ➤ *pp. 125-126*

1. Select the list and open the Properties dialog box (right-click and select List Properties).
2. In the List area, choose Numbered List in the Style drop-down list.
3. In the Starting number box located below the Number style drop-down list, type the number you want to start with.

habits & strategies

Lists are easier to read and understand when each item in the list begins or is phrased the same way. Using Netscape Editor, you can format and enhance lists in all sorts of ways.

Lists are one of the most common ways of organizing information in a Web document. Lists are sometimes easier to read than paragraphs. They are well suited for communicating various and sundry facts, instructions, and ideas.

You often see a list being used to make a table of contents at the beginning of a long Web page. Each item in the table of contents list is linked to a section of the document so that readers can access the entire page from the first screen they see. (Chapter 7 explains hypertext links and how you can use them to create table of contents lists.)

Netscape Editor makes it pretty easy to create the three most popular types of lists: ordered (numbered) lists, unordered (bulleted) lists, and definition lists. You can also put one list inside another to create what are called "nested lists." And, if you're so inclined, you can fool with the numbering scheme of lists and even get bullets of different shapes and sizes.

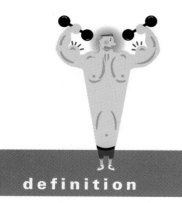

definition

definition list : *A list, such as a glossary, consisting of pairs of entries, with a term and its definition making up each pair.*

trends

It's hard to imagine the basic functions of lists changing much beyond what we see already. But changing the way we select from sets of data is sure to evolve. One thing lacking from a current static list mentality is the ability to offer a nonlinear or dynamic list. One might, for example, want to treat catalogs of icons or images as list entities. Scripts and servers that can treat list data as "objects" from a database should add a new twist to lists—letting the end user re-sort lists alphabetically, say, or based on any "category field" defined in the pages. For example, the modeling of list selections in 3D graphical space is already creating a small revolution in the conversion of gopher server menus into 3D icons. We may see templates on the server or client side creating custom views of list items as doors in a hallway, stores in a mall, CDs in a bookshelf, or trees in a forest.

One list feature that Netscape Editor does not support is called "compact." In HTML, a list can be specified as compact, telling the browser to display it in as little space as possible.

THE THREE WAYS TO MAKE LISTS

Netscape Editor gives you three different ways to create lists. After you have experimented with all three methods, you will discover which method works most comfortably for you.

- Perhaps the easiest way to make a list is to "turn on" the list formatting and then type the list items, pressing ENTER at the end of each line. With this technique, Netscape Editor formats the list for you as you complete each list entry.
- You can also type the list items first (and put each item in a separate paragraph). When you're done, select the entire list and *then* choose the list format you want for the items.
- The third way is to right-click (on the Mac, click and hold down the mouse button) on a list item, choose Paragraph I List Properties from the menu that pops up, and select the list format you want from the Properties dialog box.

UNORDERED (BULLET) LISTS

A bulleted list is one in which each item begins with a filled-in black circle called a *bullet.* To make a bulleted list you don't have to type the bullet symbols because the Web browser (or Netscape Editor) does that for you. To start typing a "bullet list" (as Netscape calls them), click the Bullet List button.

Bullet List

Netscape inserts the first bullet. Type the first item in the list and press ENTER when you are done. Netscape inserts a bullet at the start of the second line. Type the second item on the list, press ENTER, and repeat as often as necessary (see Figure 6.1).

When you get to the end of the list, press ENTER one more time. Netscape inserts one more bullet than you want, but don't worry about that. Just click the Bullet List button again to "unpush" it. The last bullet disappears and the line that the cursor is on returns to normal paragraph formatting.

As you type a bulleted list, the Bullet List button appears to be "pushed in." If you ever have any doubts about what kind of list you're creating, you can always glance at the buttons.

You can also create a bulleted list by typing the items as you would regular paragraphs. When you're done writing the list, select all the paragraphs you wrote and click the Bullet List button. This technique works just as well.

If you want to reassure yourself that your lists are being numbered correctly, preview your document by clicking the View in Browser button.

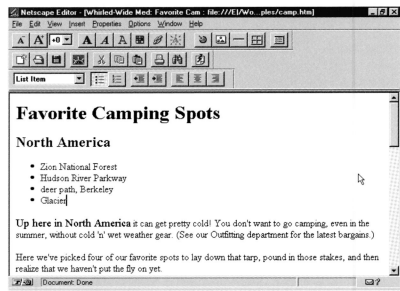

Figure 6.1 A bullet list being created.

ORDERED (NUMBERED) LISTS

To make a numbered list, you don't actually type the numbers. The Web browser that displays your document creates them on the fly. In Netscape Editor, the numbers are represented by two dummy characters (##), also called *hash marks*. Upcoming versions of Navigator Gold may do away with this "feature" but for now, it's easier for Netscape Editor to handle numbered lists if it doesn't have to recalculate the numbers constantly. Don't worry, your Web document will have real numbering in it when viewed with any Web browser.

To create a numbered list, start by clicking the Numbered List button. Notice how this button appears to be "pushed in." As long as the Numbered List button has been selected, the text you type will be numbered.

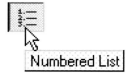

Netscape inserts the first hash marks. Type the first item in the list and press ENTER when you're done. Netscape inserts another hash mark on the next line. Type the next line of the list and repeat as often as necessary (see Figure 6.2).

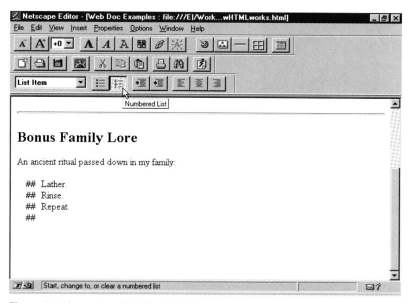

Figure 6.2 A numbered list in progress.

When you get to the end of the list, press ENTER one more time. Netscape will insert one more set of hash marks than you want, but this is a simple problem to solve. Just click the Numbered List button again. Now the button appears to be "unpushed." The hash marks disappear and the line where the cursor is returns to normal paragraph formatting.

Another way to type a numbered list is to type the items as you would regular paragraphs, and when you're done, select the list and click the Numbered List button.

If you need to interrupt a numbered list by putting a normal paragraph between two numbered items, see the "Special List Formatting" section later in this chapter.

DEFINITION LISTS

Definition lists are technically designed for glossaries, itineraries, and other documents in which single items are associated with lengthy descriptions. Browsers display definition lists in different ways. Sometimes the lists are displayed in two columns, with the items in the first column and the definitions in the second. In general, definition lists are more commonly displayed on separate lines, with the definitions indented. Figure 6.3 shows a short description list created with Netscape Editor.

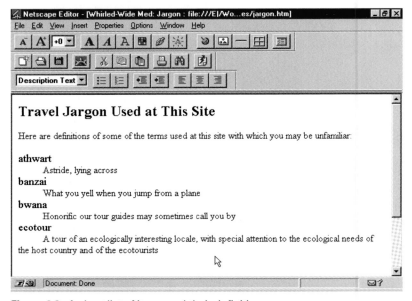

Figure 6.3 A short list of items and their definitions.

Netscape refers to definition lists as "description lists" for reasons we can't fathom. The program also does not create the HTML for these lists correctly (unless you tinker with the Properties dialog box and select the Description List style, but that's not particularly convenient). For the record, it leaves off the beginning and ending list tags. To be fair, we should say that Netscape Editor doesn't create definition lists correctly for all browsers—but, any definition list you create with Netscape Editor looks fine in Netscape Navigator, naturally.

Two types of entries appear in definition lists—definition terms and the definitions themselves. Netscape calls the terms *description titles* and the definitions *description text*. Whatever.

There are two ways to mark a paragraph as a description title. Either pull down the Paragraph style drop-down list, choose Description

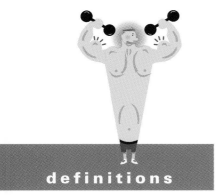

directory list: A directory list is a list of files in a directory (folder), some other analogous list of contents, or entries in any other kind of directory (such as a phone directory). Most browsers render directory lists in the same way as unordered lists (that is, with bullets).

menu list: A menu list is a list of choices, such as a list of hypertext links to various information sources. Most browsers render menu lists the same as unordered lists as well (yes, with bullets).

Title and begin typing the paragraph, or select an existing paragraph, pull down the Paragraph style drop-down list and choose Description Title

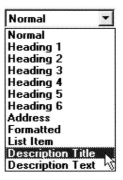

Similarly, to mark a paragraph as description text, pull down the Paragraph style drop-down list, choose Description Text and start typing. Or, select an existing paragraph first, then pull down the Paragraph style drop-down list and choose Description Text.

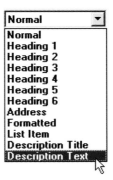

OTHER KINDS OF LISTS

Netscape Editor offers two other types of lists that you may occasionally want to create—directory lists and menu lists. However, most browsers display these lists exactly the same way they display unordered lists (as single-column bulleted lists). That's how Netscape displays them and that's how they look in Netscape Editor. You can't press a button to create a directory or menu list, nor can you choose a

style from the Paragraph style drop-down list. Instead, you have to enter the text, select the text, and then choose the list command that converts the text into the kind of list you want. After you've selected the text, you can either right-click and choose Paragraph | List Properties or else select Properties | Text from the menus. At this point you see the Properties dialog box (see Figure 6.4).

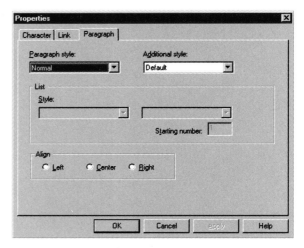

Figure 6.4 The Paragraph tab of the Properties dialog box has all the controls for lists.

Choose List Item in the Paragraph style drop-down list, even if it's already selected, so that the Style drop-down list in the List selection becomes active (that is, it turns white instead of gray).

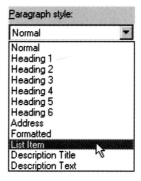

Choose either Menu List or Directory List from the Style drop-down list. Then click OK.

SPECIAL LIST FORMATTING

Besides bulleted, numbered, and definition lists, Netscape Editor offers one or two additional tricks you can do with lists.

Lists Within Lists

It's possible to include a list within a list. Such lists are called nested lists. A list that appears within the same type of list, such as a bullet list within a bullet list, is an example of a nested list. One type of list can also be nested inside another type of list (see Figure 6.5).

If you're typing the list from scratch and you want to "nest" bullets under bullets or numbers under numbers, click the Increase Indent button when you get to the first item you want to be subordinate.

The item will be indented further. In the case of a bullet list, a different type of bullet appears beside the nested items.

If you want to change the subordinate, or nested, list from bullets to numbers or from numbers to bullets, click the Bullet List or Numbered List button. To get a subordinate directory list or menu list, select a definition list style from the Paragraph style drop-down list, or go to the Properties dialog box and apply one of its esoteric list styles.

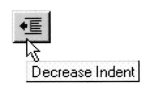

If you change your mind about a subordinate list, you can click the Decrease Indent button to reverse the indentation process.

habits & strategies

You may notice that some Web pages feature unordered lists with little colored ball graphics instead of bullets. Usually, these are not actual lists but simply sequences of paragraphs, each starting with the same graphical figure (such as the dingbats offered by Netscape's Page Wizard, as discussed in Chapter 4). For more on how to insert any type of graphic into a page, see Chapter 8.

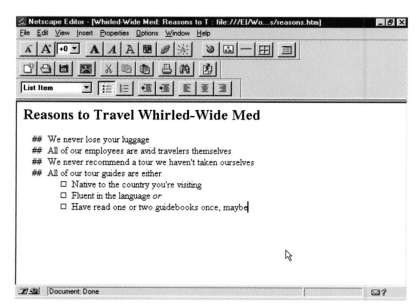

Figure 6.5 An example of a list within a list.

Changing the Bullet Type or Numbering Scheme

When you nest a bullet list, each new level gets a different bullet (at least until you run through the four types of bullets).

But it's also possible to choose a bullet type for bullets at any level. Similarly, you can choose a different numbering scheme for numbered lists.

To see the bullet options available to you, select a list and go to the Properties dialog box. In the List area's Style drop-down list, choose Unnumbered List (notice that Netscape is not consistent about this nomenclature: unordered list, bullet list, unnumbered list). Then, in the Bullet style drop-down list to the right, choose Automatic, Solid circle, Solid square, or Open square.

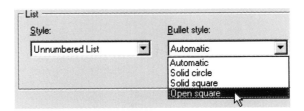

To see the numbering options available to you, select a list and go to the Properties dialog box. In the List area, choose Numbered List in the Style drop-down list. Then, in the Number style drop-down list to the right, choose Automatic; 1,2,3...; I,II,III...; A,B,C...; or a,b,c....

Netscape Navigator can also display lower-case roman numerals (i, ii, iii), but Netscape Editor currently can't make them.

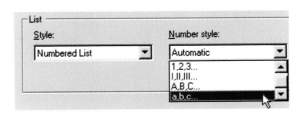

Restarting Numbering

Suppose you want to interrupt a numbered list with one or two paragraphs of commentary. You type the first few entries in the list, click the Number List button ("unpush" it), type the commentary paragraphs, and then click the Number List button (so it looks pushed-in again) to resume the numbered list again. However, instead of starting where you left off, the second part of the list begins with the number 1 (see Figure 6.6).

Fortunately, you can control how a list is numbered. You can number lists continuously even when one or two paragraphs appear between the numbered items. You can even start a list with a numeral other than 1.

CAUTION

These bullet and numbering style options are all Netscape-specific and will be ignored by most other Web browsers.

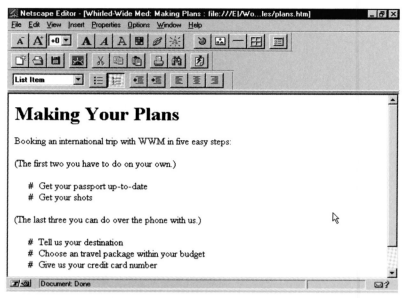

Figure 6.6 Two numbered lists separated by an intervening paragraph.

To start numbering a list with a number other than 1, select the list and go to the Properties dialog box. In the List area, choose Numbered List in the Style drop-down list. Then, in the Starting number box (you'll find it below the Number style drop-down list), type the number you want to start with.

Remember, you won't see the numbers at all unless you preview the document in the Web browser.

CAUTION

Starting a list with a number other than 1 is a Netscape extension to basic HTML and will not be interpreted correctly by most other browsers.

OTHER PRESENTATION AND LAYOUT IDEAS

If lists don't quite do it for you as far as laying out the information in your document, you might want to look into a couple of other formatting techniques. Tables (covered in Chapter 10) enable you to place columns of text side-by-side (among other things). Preformatted text, which you've already seen how to create, can be used to place characters precisely where you want them.

For more ambitious or elaborate layout and navigation plans, you might want to employ frames (explained in Chapter 12).

WHAT'S NEXT?

You now know enough to create, edit, and format Web documents. The next step is linking them together to create a Web site your readers can navigate easily. The next chapter will show you how to create and manage hyperlinks. After that (in Chapters 8 and 9), we'll show you how to incorporate illustrations and other media into your Web presentations. In Chapters 10 and 11, you'll learn how to create sophisticated page layouts with tables and how to incorporate elements for other browsers, even when Netscape Editor can't do it for you.

CHAPTER 7

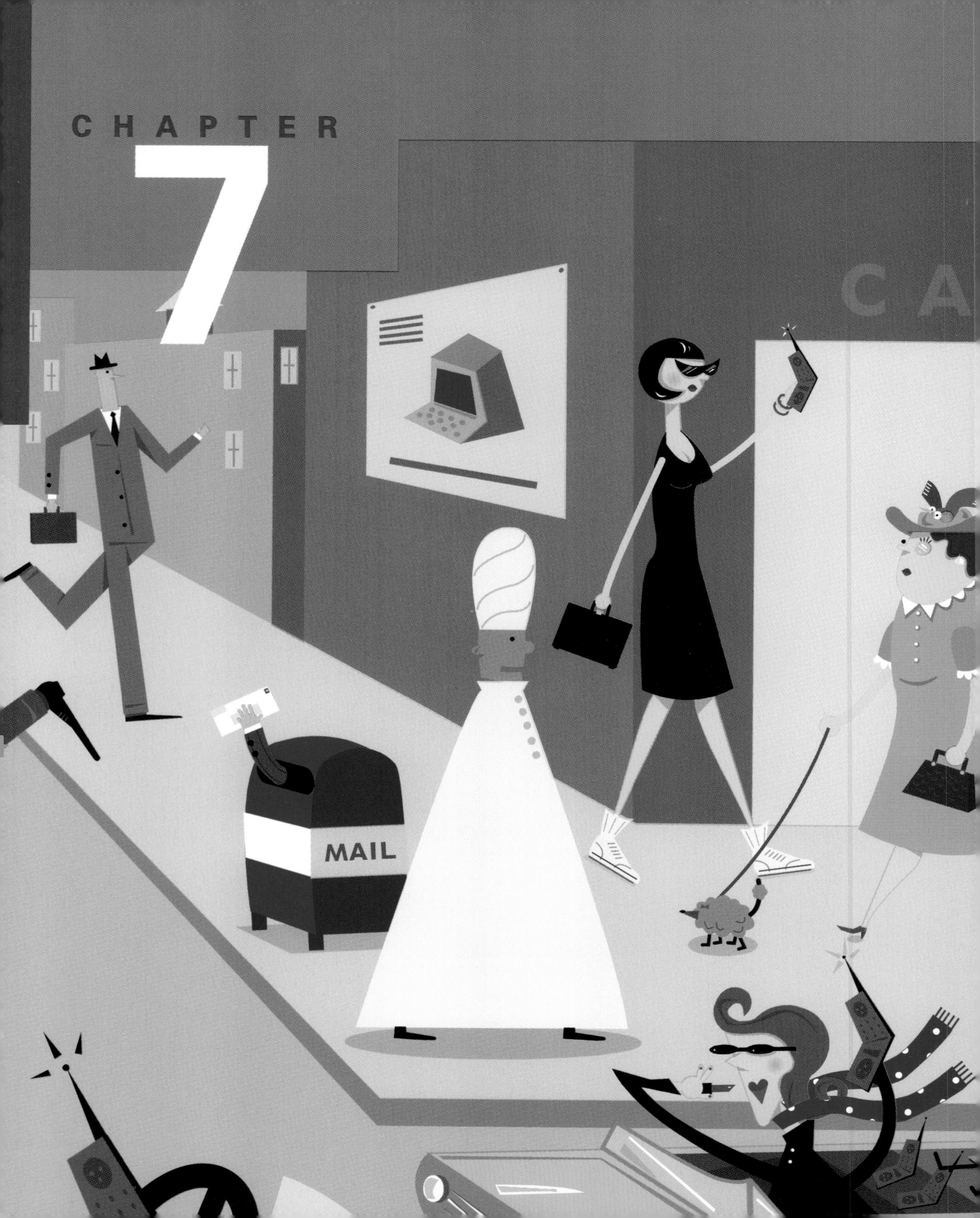

Inserting Hyperlinks

FAST FORWARD

North America

- Zion National Forest
- Hudson River Parkway
- deer path, Berkeley
- Glacier

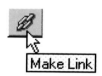

THERE ARE TWO ENDS TO A LINK ➤ *p. 132*

They are
1. The hyper-reference (link) anchor *and*
2. The target of the link, which can be
   - a named anchor within a document *or*
   - another document *or*
   - some other Internet resource

LINKS PROVIDE ORGANIZATION
TO THE PAGES AT A WEB SITE ➤ *pp. 132-133*

- They help readers navigate from one page to another.
- They make it possible for the home page to always be a single jump from a page at the site.

INSERT A HYPERLINK ➤ *pp. 135-137*

1. Select text.
2. Click the Make Link button.

SAVE YOUR DOCUMENT
(IF YOU HAVEN'T YET) ➤ *p. 138*

1. Click the Save button.
2. Save the document.

MAKE AN INTERNAL (LOCAL) LINK ➤ *pp. 137-139*

1. If you know the name of the local file you want to link to and if it's in the same folder (directory) as the document you're working on, then just type the filename directly into the Link to a page location or local file box.
2. Otherwise, click the Browse File button.
3. Browse around looking for the file you want and then click Open.
4. Click OK.

Link to

Link to a page location or local file:

http://www.sito.org

MAKE AN EXTERNAL (REMOTE) LINK ➤ *pp. 143-146*

1. Type, or paste, the URL directly into the Link to a page location or local file box.
2. Then click OK.

DRAG A LINK ONTO YOUR PAGE ➤ *pp. 146-147*

1. Switch to the Netscape Navigator Web browser (or select File I New Web Browser if you only have a Netscape Editor window open at the time).
2. Find your way to the document you want to link to.
3. Reduce the size of the Navigator window so that you can also see part of the Editor window showing the portion of the document where you want to insert the link.
4. Click the Link icon to the left of the Location box (and hold down the mouse button).
5. Drag over to the Editor window.
6. Position the pointer where you want the new link to appear and then release the mouse button.

Once you've been around the Web even a short while, you should have some passing familiarity with the concept of hyperlinks and how they work. Generally, in a browser such as Navigator, you click the highlighted (and usually underlined) word, and you are instantly "taken" to another document (or to another location in the same document, or to some other type of object entirely) or something happens (such as a sound or movie playing). Of course, you aren't literally taken anywhere. Your browser just reaches out across the Net and grabs the thing you asked for.

But you didn't really ask for anything, at least not by name, did you? No, you just clicked on (or selected) a link of some kind. The browser did the rest. For this immediate and invisible response to your wordless request to actually work, somebody had to embed the hyperlink in the document. In this chapter, we'll show you how to insert such hyperlinks into your document with Netscape Editor.

SOME CONCEPTUAL GROUNDING

There are two ends to each hyperlink (both of which are referred to, technically, as *anchors*). At one end is the "hot" (as in active), or hyper-, text or graphics button, usually referred to as the link. At the other end is the target of the link. The latter can be something on the same server (on the same machine) as the document containing the hyperlink, or it can be out somewhere else on the Internet, as long as it's publicly readable and accessible via the World Wide Web.

Sensible Linking

In planning out the hyperlinked organization of your Web site, you have to give your visitors some reasonably understandable routes or pathways through your site. You also want to make sure that they can

If you're comfortable with your grasp of hyperlinks, what they are and what they do, then you can skip ahead to the next section. (You don't have to, but you'll probably want to.)

button: Some people refer to all hyperlinks as buttons, but it's also possible to create graphic images that resemble real, pushable buttons, and then use them as standardized links (such as "Back" and "Forward").

By the way, hyperlinks can also be formatted with all the normal text formatting features (see Chapter 5). So, for example, headings can be hyperlinks, as can items in bulleted lists, addresses, and so on.

easily get back to the home page from anywhere within the site. People browsing the Net can generally use their Back buttons to retrace their steps, but if they jumped directly into somewhere in the middle of your site, they won't automatically have any easy way of returning to a preceding page. When you're planning your site, you will want to organize the folders (if there are more than one) into a conceptual hierarchy. Similarly, as people follow links deeper and deeper into your site, you'll want to make sure they can easily work their way back to the "surface" whenever they feel the need to.

Figure 7.1 shows a diagram describing the layout of the major sections of a Web site. The home page links to a number of subordinate pages, all of which link back to the home page, and many of which link to further specialized pages.

Another useful application of hyperlinking is to include a table of contents at the top of a long document, usually consisting of the major headings in the document (perhaps in the format of a bulleted list, as explained in Chapter 6). Each of the headings in the table of contents can then be a hyperlink to the section it names, giving the reader an

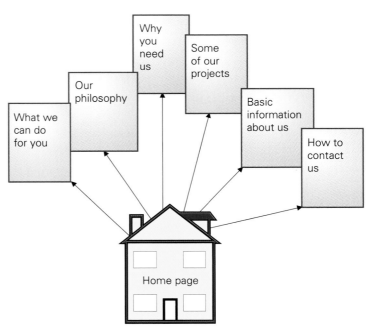

Figure 7.1 The conceptual layout of a company's Web site

Try to avoid the "click here" cliché, as in "To see my cool links, click **here**." Not only is this meaningless to people using nongraphical browsers, such as Lynx (because they don't click anything), but it also reads like comic book hype. Instead, try normal English: "I've collected all my favorite **cool links** on one page."

For more on inserting graphics into Web documents, see Chapter 8.

easy way to jump directly to the part of the document he or she is interested in (see Figure 7.2).

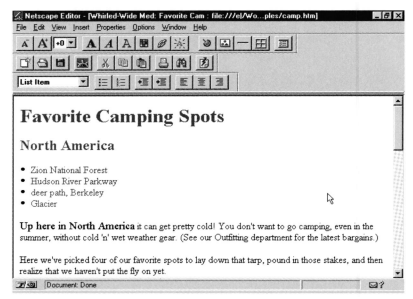

Figure 7.2 This sample camping page from the Whirled-Wide Med site features hyperlinks at the top of the document linking to each of the sections below

Select Text, Then Make It into an Anchor

The usual approach to making hyperlinks is to type the text (or insert the graphics) into the document first, and *then* select the salient text (or image) and associate a link with it. Some links require formalized text (such as "Next page" or "Table of contents") as part of an overall design, often at the head or foot of, or at regular locations within, a Web page. Other links are embedded into the normal flow of the text, directly in context, such as it were (see Figure 7.3).

A Little More About Anchors

There are two kinds of anchors. One can be referred to as a hyper-reference (from the HTML command HREF used to specify it) but

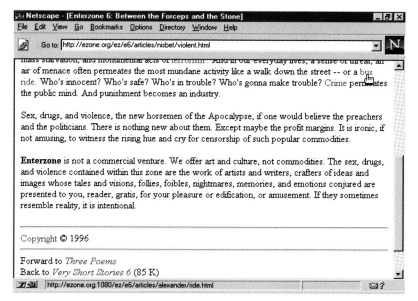

Figure 7.3 This Web page (from *Enterzone*) shows some regular organizational hyperlinks along with some "digressive" links that lead directly out of the main body of the text

is usually just called a link. The hyper-reference defines the "hot" text. The other kind of anchor is a target, also called a name (from the HTML command NAME that defines it), or a named anchor. A named anchor defines a point in or section of a document to which a hyper- reference may link directly. Figure 7.4 shows a simple diagram of a link between two anchors in two separate documents.

Named anchors are not required for hyperlinks! Linking to a document without specifying a named anchor will automatically land you at the beginning of the document.

HOW TO ACTUALLY DO IT

With Netscape Editor, inserting hyperlinks is simply a matter of selecting text and then clicking the Make Link button or dragging a link (or a local document) directly into the Web document you're working on. Before putting the links into your document, get all the writing done. Write your first draft, edit it, and format it (as explained in Chapter 5)

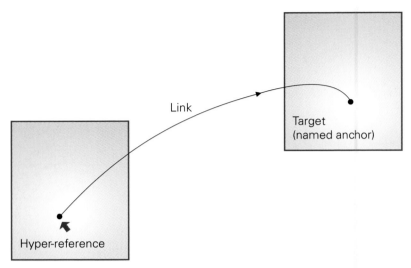

Figure 7.4 A link has two anchors: the hyper-reference (where you click, in Netscape) and the target (where you end up). The target can be a named anchor or, by default, the beginning of the linked document

until it looks good and *then* put the links in. (You can still edit or change it *after* you've inserted the hyperlinks, if you need to.)

There are two different broad categories of links, by the way, usually referred to as internal or external links. Internal links connect to documents (or objects) located on the same computer (the same server) as the document the link is in. External links connect to documents (or objects) located somewhere else on the Net. These are also sometimes referred to as relative or absolute links, because internal links can be identified relative to the location of the starting document, whereas external links must be identified by complete Web addresses (URLs). Figure 7.5 shows a document with relative internal links and absolute external links.

Select the Text for the Link

No matter what kind of link you're about to insert, you usually do so by first selecting the text you want to be "active." (Selecting text is explained in Chapter 5.)

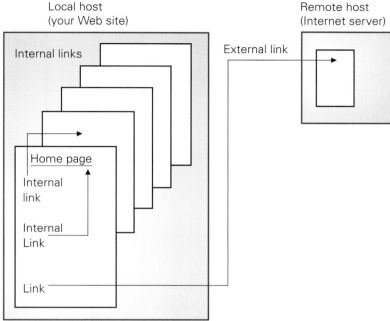

Figure 7.5 The main document links to other documents at this site as well as to resources at other sites out there on the Net

Select text first when you know the location of the object you're linking to or can find it on your own computer. If you want to drag a link from the Web browser to a document in the Editor, it will come with its own suggested text, which you can edit, if necessary.

With formal, organized links, such as links from each entry in a table of contents to the referred articles, the text to choose is obvious. With "in context" links, you'll have some choice about what text to select and treat as a link. Figure 7.6 shows a rather poor choice for hypertext along with a better choice.

If you like, you can also just position the insertion point and then go ahead to the next step. If no text is selected, you'll be able to type in text for your link when you select the document you're linking to.

Internal, or Relative, Hyperlinks

Once you've selected text, click the Make Link button.

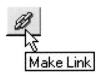

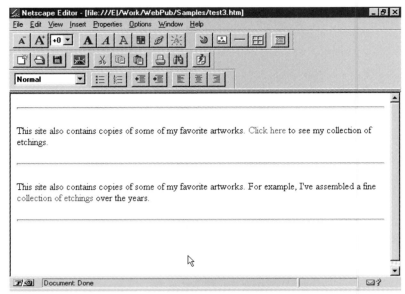

Figure 7.6 The active hyperlink text should consist of words that make sense leading to the anchor in question

The first time you try to insert a link into a document using any method, Netscape will prompt you to save the document you're working on.

habits & strategies

As a shortcut, after selecting the text you want to make into a link, you can right-click on it (for the Mac, click and hold down the mouse button) and then select Create link using selection. This will bring up the Properties dialog box with its Link tab selected.

If you haven't saved the current document yet, Netscape Editor will prompt you to do so:

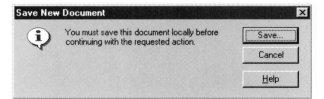

Click the Save button and then save the document. This brings up the Properties dialog box with the Link tab selected (see Figure 7.7).

If you know the name of the local file you want to link to and if it's in the same folder (directory) as the document you're working on, then you can just type the filename directly into the Link to a page location or local file box. Otherwise, click the Browse File button.

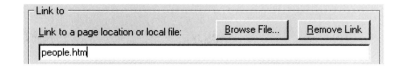

This brings up the Link to File dialog box, a dead-ringer for the normal Open dialog box. Browse around looking for the file you want and then click Open. The path leading to the file you want will tell the browser how to find it *relative* to the location of the current document.

Then click OK. The text you selected will appear in your preferred link color (or perhaps in your "visited link" color, if you've displayed the linked document recently). The link won't function in Netscape Editor (except that you *can* right-click—or click and hold down on the Mac—and select Browse to (*the name of the file*) or Open link in Editor, depending on whether you just want to see the linked file or edit it.

CAUTION

Make sure you put the files you want to link to in the folders you'll eventually want them in (such as in the same folder as the main document or in a subfolder), because if you move them later relative to the main document, the links will fail to work.

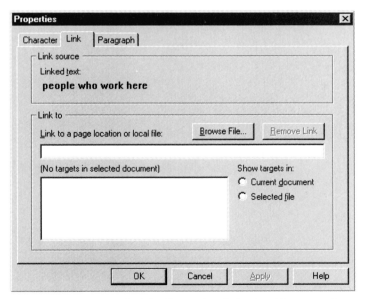

Figure 7.7 From the Link tab of the Properties dialog box it's easy to insert a hyperlink

*To see the name of such an
anchor, place the mouse pointer
over the Target icon. The name
of the anchor will appear in the
status bar.*

Inserting Named Anchors

Earlier, we mentioned the idea of named anchors, which are marked
sections of a document to which you can link directly. Just as you must
create a document before you can link to it (or at least before you can
find it by browsing to insert a link to it), you must also create any names
before you can link directly to them.

To insert a named anchor into a document, first select the text
you want to name (think of it as a target for a hyperlink). Then click the
Insert Target (Named Anchor) button.

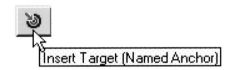

This brings up the Target Properties dialog box with a suggested
name for the anchor (the selected text itself or at least the first 255
characters of it). Shorten the name or change it to something more
memorable, if you want, and then click OK. Netscape Editor inserts a
Target icon at the beginning of the named anchor to remind you that
it's there.

Legal  Stuff

Linking to a Named Anchor

For any document with named anchors in it, you can link either directly
to the document or to one of the names. You can also link to any named
anchor in the current document (this is the usual way tables of contents
are made). To do so, select the text and click the Make Link button to
bring up the Link tab of the Properties dialog box. The Select a named
target in current document box will display any names in the document
you're editing (see Figure 7.8).

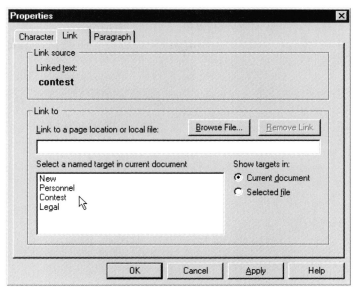

Figure 7.8 You can link to a named anchor by selecting it from a list

To link to a name in the current document, click one of the listed names. It will appear (preceded by a #) in the Link to a page location or local file box.

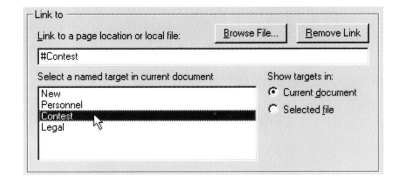

To link to a named anchor in a local document, first click the Browse File button and select the document you want, as explained in

habits & strategies

You can also drag a file directly from a folder window on your computer screen onto a Web page you're editing. See "Dragging Links onto Your Page," in the section coming up.

the previous section. Any names in that document will then appear in the named target list, and the radio button to its right will move from the Current document position to the Selected file choice (see Figure 7.9).

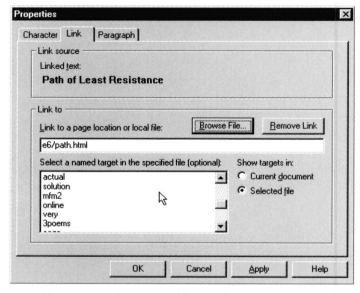

Figure 7.9 If you link to a document with named anchors in it, you can select one of the names to focus your link even further

Click the name you want. It will be added to the filename (separated by a # character).

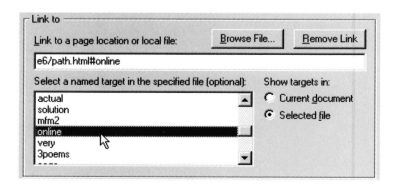

CAUTION

The addresses of documents on other people's Web sites can change at any time without notice. As soon as you start building pages that link to other sites, you've also taken on a long-term project of maintaining those links and keeping them up to date.

*People can easily get confused
about where they are when
browsing the Web. If you offer
links that take readers away
from your site, you may want to
alert them to the fact with some
equivalent of a "Now Leaving
Kansas" sign or even an
explanation that you have no
control over the content of the
linked sites.*

*To embed a live e-mail link
into a page, link to mailto:
e-mail.address (as in
mailto:xian@syx.com).*

External, or Absolute, Hyperlinks

Most Web sites have some links to other sites. Otherwise, the
site will be a sort of island in cyberspace. If you want other people to
link into your site, you have to be willing to reciprocate and offer links
from your site to others'. Most of the time, you'll want to do this anyway.
Hardly anyone on the Net doesn't have a few favorite sites or sources
for useful tools or information relative to whatever they're putting up
on their own Web pages.

External links are essentially the same as internal links, except the
reference to the linked page has to be a complete URL, rather than just
a filename or a relative path and a filename.

A URL Refresher Course

If you remember what URLs are and how to type them, then you can
skip to the next section. Fortunately, most of the links you'll be inserting
into your pages will already exist in some electronic form (in e-mail
people have sent to you, in your bookmarks file, or on other people's
Web pages), so you hardly ever *have to* type URLs, if you don't want
to. On the other hand, it can often be faster to just type 'em in directly,
rather than rooting around on your computer or out there on the Net for
an address.

URLs start with a protocol, which is *http://* nine times out of ten
(other likely protocols are *ftp://*, *gopher://*, *mailto:*, and *telnet://*). Next
comes the actual Internet address of the site hosting the document
you're referring to. It's usually one or two words separated by dots,
either *hostname.subdomain.domain* or just *subdomain.domain*. After
that, somewhat rarely, there can be a colon and a port number (such as
:1080). A URL can end right there, if you want to refer to the primary
document at a Web site (the root, or home page of the site). Then there
can be a forward slash followed by either a path (if the document you're
referring to is not in the root directory of the Web server), a path and a
filename (if the file you're looking for is not the default one at the folder
referred to in the path), or just a filename.

But these are all just technicalities you need to have straight when
you're typing these long URLs in. Once they're embedded into documents (yours or others), it becomes a matter of clicking links. The true

power of the Web is that you *can* embed a reference to just about any type of resource out there on the Net, and your browser will try to haul back whatever you've linked to for you.

bookmark

*For more on how to form Web addresses, see the official documents at the W3 headquarters (**www.w3.org/pub/WWW/Addressing**).*

Table 7.1 shows a smattering of URLs drawn from our bookmarks, so you can see how all the variations fall into the same format.

Resource Name	URL
BrowserWatch	**http://www.browserwatch.com/**
Net Legends FAQ	**gopher://dixie.aiss.uiuc.edu:6969/00/urban.legends/net.legends/ Net.Legends.FAQ**
BIGGEST WEB BLUNDERS	**http://www.gigaplex.com/wow/10top/10blund.htm**
Netscape download site	**ftp://ftp2.netscape.com/**
Busy Person's Links	**http://syx.com/x/busy/**

Table 7.1 Some URLs

Typing in External Links Directly

You still start by selecting the text you want to use as the hyperlink. Then click the Make Link button (or right-click—or hold down the mouse button, for Macs—and select Create link using selected). This brings up the Properties dialog box with the Link tab selected, as shown in Figure 7.7.

Now type, or paste, the URL directly into the Link to a page location or local file box.

Link to

Link to a page location or local file: [Browse File...] [Remove Link]

http://www.sito.org

habits & strategies

If you have the URL handy in some other document (in another program, say), go ahead and select it in that other document and copy it. Then, instead of typing it when the time comes, you can just paste it in.

trends

The next step beyond URL are URNs (Uniform Resource Names). The standards haven't been worked out, but in principle, a URN would identify each unique object on the Net. Then it wouldn't matter if specific objects were moved from place to place, since their names would not depend on their "addresses." Another direction the Web might go in is toward the Hyper-G format. Hyper-G is a sort of super-WWW standard that demands much more from its servers. When surfing "Hyper-G" space, your client software makes requests of its host server, which is largely a huge database of information about objects on the Net. Your server contacts other servers as needed, sharing information much as libraries lend each other books. We haven't seen any mass movement toward Hyper-G though, but you heard it here first.

Then click OK. Figure 7-10 shows a portion of a document with a series of external links.

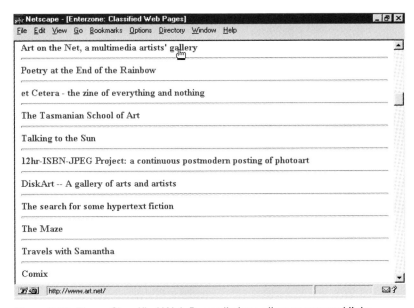

Figure 7.10 These Classified Web Pages listings all go to external links

Linking to a Named Anchor

To link to a named anchor within a document at an external site, the process is almost the same. You still select the text you want to use as a link and bring up the Properties dialog box with the Link tab selected. You still enter or paste in the address of the document in question.

Then, to specify a name, type a pound sign (#) after the address and then the text of the name itself:

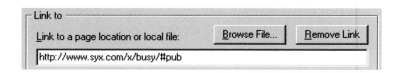

Then click OK.

Dragging Links onto Your Page

If you *don't* have the exact text of a URL handy at your fingertips, it's easy enough to drag it from the Web itself (or from any page that contains a link to the address you want). To do so, first switch to the Netscape Navigator Web browser (or select File I New Web Browser if you only have a Netscape Editor window open at the time). Then find your way to the document you want to link to. How do you do that without knowing the address? Well, how do you ever find *anything* on the Web? Go to your bookmarks, or follow links that will help you get there in several steps, or even search for the site with one of the search engines listed on Netscape's Search page (select Directory I Internet Search in the Navigator window).

If you get to the exact page you want, first reduce the size of the Navigator window so that you can also see part of the Editor window showing the portion of the document where you want to insert the link. Then click the Link icon to the left of the Location box and hold down the mouse button.

habits & strategies

You can also drag local files into your documents to produce hyperlinks to them. Just open the folder containing the file you want to link to, select the icon for the document in question, and drag it onto the Editor window to the place you want to insert the link.

Your Netscape bookmarks are contained in a document called bookmark.htm (or Bookmarks.html). If you browse to that file (we sometimes use ours as a starting home page), then you can copy any of its links for insertion into other documents.

Drag over to the Editor window. You'll see the mouse pointer turn into a special Insert Link icon.

More Web Resources

Position the pointer where you want the new link to appear and then release the mouse button. The link will appear in the document, with a guess for the link text. Netscape will guess the title of the document you've linked to for actual Web documents (a good guess) or the URL of any other kind of file (probably not what you'd want in the long run, but suitable as a placeholder).

If you find the acrobatics of positioning the two windows, clicking, and dragging a little too complicated (and we wouldn't blame you), you can also just double-click the Link icon. This places the address of the current page on your clipboard, suitable for pasting. Then just switch to the Editor window, position the mouse pointer and press CTRL-V (COMMAND-V on the Mac) to insert the link.

Copying Links from Any Web Document

Another way to insert a link into the document you're working on is to copy it from an existing page. To do so, just right-click on an existing link and select Copy link to clipboard from the menu that pops up.

Then return to the document you're editing, position the insertion point, and press CTRL-V. For link text, Netscape Editor will suggest the address or path and filename of the copied link.

Editing Link Text

If you want to overrule Netscape's suggestion for the link text, just click at the beginning of the link (place the insertion point just *before* the first letter of the link text), type new text, and *then* delete the original text.

REMOVING A LINK

If you ever create a link by mistake or in the wrong place, you can remove it easily. Just right-click on the link (yes, or with a Mac, click and hold down), and then select Remove Link. There's also a Remove Link command on the Link tab of the Properties dialog box, if you happen to have it open already.

IMAGES AS HYPERLINKS

As mentioned earlier in this chapter, graphic images can also be turned into hyperlinks. (The process is the same, except you must select the graphic first, instead of text, before assigning the link.) For more on inserting images, see Chapter 8.

Another common form of hyperlink is something called an image map. An image map is a graphic with links to several different anchors, depending on where the graphic is clicked (that's the "map" part, because the graphic can be thought of as a map of various regions, all leading to different destinations). The areas of the map that send you to different targets are sometimes referred to as "hot spots." Image maps are often used at the bottom of every page of a site, as an attractive, ubiquitous navigation aid. See Chapter 12 for several ways to create image maps.

WHAT'S NEXT?

The Web would never be as popular as it is today if it weren't for the ability to include images in Web site design. Chapter 8 will tell you the do's and don'ts of graphic images on the Web and show you how to pull art onto your pages with ease using Netscape Editor.

Illustrating Your Pages with Eye-Grabbing Graphics

FAST FORWARD

GRAPHICS FORMATS THAT
WORK ON THE WEB ➤ *pp. 156-159*
There are only two graphics formats widely viewable on the Web:
- GIF, which is generally better for solid-color images with limited palettes, *and*
- JPEG, which is generally better for color photographs.

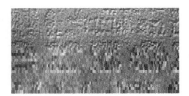

INTERLACE YOUR GIFS ➤ *pp. 158-159*
Interlaced GIFs appear to load faster, since they are sketched in at first, based on a small fraction of the entire image.

TWO WAYS TO CREATE GRAPHICS ➤ *pp. 159-160*
- "Draw" the art yourself, using a drafting and art program, creating it from scratch with the computer.
- Scan existing photography or line art and then manipulate it or reproduce it as close to the original as possible.

CONVERT EXISTING GRAPHICS ➤ *pp. 161-162*
1. Some scanner software can save images as both GIFs and JPEGs.
2. If you have a program that can convert between GIFs and JPEGs, you just need to be able to get existing images into one of those formats to have both options.

Insert Image

Image file name
splashhi.jpg

Alternative representations (optional):

I̲mage: splashlo.jpg

Te̲xt: [Our founder, in a casual moment]

Link source

Linked image:
file:///E|/Work/WebPub/Samples/splashhi.jpg

INSERT GRAPHICS INTO PAGES ➤ *pp. 162-163*

1. Before inserting a graphic, place the insertion point where you want it to appear.
2. Click the Insert Image button.
3. If you haven't saved your document yet, Netscape Editor will prompt you to do so.
4. Type the path and file name of the image, if you know it (or click the Browse button to the right of the Image file name box, find the file you want in the Select Image File dialog box, and then click the Open button).
5. Click OK.

PROVIDE ALTERNATIVE TEXT FOR IMAGES ➤ *p. 164*

While still in the Image Properties dialog box, after specifying an image file,

1. Click in the Alternative Text box.
2. Type some alternative text to explain the image to those who can't see it (or type " " if you want nothing to display in place of the image).

MAKE A GRAPHIC INTO A LINK ➤ *pp. 167-168*

1. If you want the graphic you're inserting to function as a link—the same way text links (described in Chapter 7) do—then click the Link tab on the Properties dialog box.
2. Type a page location (for an external document) or click the Browse button to choose a document from your local site-in-development.
3. Click OK.

DRAG GRAPHICS ONTO PAGES ➤ *pp. 168-170*

1. Open the folder containing your graphic.
2. Get your document in Netscape Editor on the screen behind the folder.
3. Drag the image icon onto the document-editing area.

153

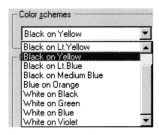

CHANGE THE COLOR
SCHEME OF A PAGE ➤ *pp. 171-175*

1. Select Properties I Document.
2. Click the Appearance tab of the Document Properties dialog box.
3. Click Use custom colors.
4. To choose a predesigned color scheme, click the drop-down list box in the Color schemes area near the top of the Document Properties dialog box.
5. If you find a color scheme you like, click OK. If not, try choosing custom colors for each of the design elements, starting with the Normal Text button.
6. Clicking any of these buttons brings up the Color dialog box. To choose any of the colors, just click on its swatch and then click OK.
7. Repeat the process for each of the text elements.
8. To select a background color, just click the Choose Color button in the Background area.
9. Choose a background color and click OK.

INSERT A BACKGROUND
PATTERN ON A PAGE ➤ *pp. 175-176*

1. Click the Image File radio button in the Background area.
2. Either type the file name of the graphic you want or click the Browse button to find it on your computer. Select the file you want and click OK.

Even older, more conservative corporations like IBM and DEC are starting to exhibit more abstract and hip pages.

**habits &
strategies**

You can satisfy text-only users by including a text-only page as an alternative to a graphics-heavy or graphics-dependent page. Then again, it's more elegant to develop a design that works with or without art and doesn't require that you keep two parallel pages up to date.

Since 1994, a Web site has had to include graphics to look "state of the art." How many magazines do you know that are all text and no pictures? Graphics on pages are a big part of what made the Web so popular, humanizing the previously cold, text-oriented Internet.

Common types of graphics include custom logos, headlines and banners, buttons (that is, clickable image links), scanned photos, pie charts, and graphs. You can use graphical elements to create a visual "look" and identity for your pages. You can also use them for illustration or visual explanations.

As important as graphics are to the overall effect of a well designed Web page, you should also take care that your pages will look and function adequately when viewed as text only. Some of your audience may be using text-only Web browsers. Even if you expect the majority of your readers to use graphical browsers, such as Netscape Navigator, a lot of people do their browsing, at least initially, with automatic image loading turned off. (Also, some Web users are blind and have text-only browsers that read, or rather "speak," the content out loud.)

As a matter of course, you can and should assign alternative text to each image so that a text-only user will get the gist of its content.

DON'T TRY TO DO IT ALL YOURSELF

One of the difficulties of designing a new Web site is that one typically aims for the sort of results that have, traditionally, taken a team of writers, editors, graphic designers, and publishing production staff to produce! Even though today's busy work environment tends to require more and more from fewer and fewer resources, you wouldn't expect an administrative person in your office to produce eye-catching and effective promotional materials—that job requires writing ad copy, creating graphics, and doing all the layout and design. Put on top of that the task of running a 24 hour-a-day computer network service that can't afford to ever be down, and you start to understand why there are so many ugly Web sites. Too many people have assumed, or have been asked to do, too much.

Creating and editing good graphics can take a lot of time and expensive software and hardware (scanner) tools. The learning curve to master some of these resources is a steep mountain to climb. The two areas where you are most likely to benefit from calling in outside expertise are graphic design and the maintenance of the network or Web server (and hence your site).

Most professional sites lean heavily on one or the other of these types of expertise. Sites developed by networking whizzes often exhibit mediocre or juvenile graphics. Sites created by graphic designers often feature clumsy navigational interfaces or slow, clunky pages that take forever to get themselves together on your screen. The best sites have just the right amount of emphasis on both appearance and functionality and are usually created by well-coordinated teams.

Producing good graphics takes hours of work and research into a plethora of terminology about image-processing, fonts, layout, specific program features, and traditional and computer-specific standards of attractive and functional page design. Even experienced, computer-savvy graphic designers have to learn new skills to design for the Web—such as what graphics formats are accepted as standards, how various Web browsers display graphics, and what the practical "bandwidth" limitations (such as modem speed) of a site's intended audience might be.

WEB GRAPHICS FORMATS

Although this may change, currently there are only two graphics formats widely viewable on the Web: GIF and JPEG.

Generally, you can assume that if a Web browser can display any graphics at all, it can display GIFs and JPEGs. (Exceptions to this would include early versions of Mosaic, which could only launch an external JPEG viewer.) If you are adapting existing art, you'll need to convert it to one of those two formats. How do you decide which to use? Here are the pros and cons.

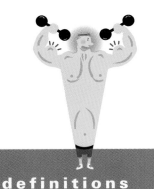

trends

When Unisys suddenly announced it had a patent that covered GIF file compression and demanded licensing fees from software vendors using GIF files (back in early 1995), the response was a backlash on the Net to move away from the GIF format. A group of folks decided to define a new, better standard. PNG (Portable Network Graphics) was the result—a new file format that included all the best features of GIF files, such as interlacing and transparency, and a non-lossy compression scheme to allow better compression than JPEG with no image-quality loss. You'd think the resulting superior file specification would have caught on quickly and that GIF and JPEG files would fade into history, but the reality is that a new format can't succeed without mass acceptance by browser vendors and Web authors. Netscape curiously ignored the PNG specs and, since they control between 60 and 80% of the browser market, PNG hasn't really caught on. Most versions of Mosaic, and just about every browser except Netscape's, seem to support PNG. Netscape instead has focused on pushing support for a little known aspect of the JPEG format called Progressive JPEG. Progressive JPEG achieves an interlaced effect by rearranging the way files load. Despite Netscape's support, this format is neither broadly supported by authoring tools nor is it backwards compatible: Progressive JPEG's can't be read at all by browsers that support only normal JPEG files. It doesn't seem likely that Progressive JPEG will ever really catch on. PNG may still have a chance, but without broad support from Netscape, it isn't likely. And with the majority of images on the Net in GIF or JPEG, it seems unlikely we'll see a fast migration to a new standard, even if it is better. Meanwhile, another JPEG variant ahs been proposed, called JPIG, but it looks like it's a long way off, something of a novelty proposed by armchair philosophers more than a likely candidate for support in the next generation of browsers and graphics programs. For more on this variant, see **http://www.algonet.se/~dip/jpig_1.htm.**

definitions

GIF: (Pronounced as in "gift" or, sometimes, "jiff.") CompuServe's Graphics Interchange Format, a standard for compressing bitmap images.

bitmap: An image composed of dots, which can be either black and white or of a palette of colors.

JPEG: (Pronounced "jaypeg.") The Joint Photographic Expert's Group's compression standard—which is a lossy standard (see next definition)—allowing a certain amount of trade-off between compression and the quality of the image.

lossy: Said of compression that "throws away" or glosses over some of the original data, for the sake of efficiency.

Pros and Cons of GIFs

GIFs can handle 256 colors, which is adequate for most graphical-illustration purposes. The amount of compression you can achieve with a GIF depends on the level of detail in your image, but you can't adjust

Don't get too hung up on trying to achieve perfect color fidelity on all platforms. It's never going to happen. Use art that will look good (or at least OK) on lower-quality platforms (such as PCs with only 16 colors).

Transparency can be tricky, because you have to choose a color that isn't being used in some other way in the image. For example, white might make a good color to turn transparent, unless there are white areas in the image that should stay opaque.

it. GIFs don't handle photographs with subtle shading gradients very well. Figure 8.1 shows an image that compresses well as a GIF.

There are two tricks you can do with GIFs that you can't do (yet) with JPEGs. The first is transparency. Most programs that can create GIFs can assign one of the colors in the palette to be transparent. This enables you to create art that appears not to have square edges.

GIFs can also be saved in an "interlaced" format, which means that a savvy browser (such as Navigator or Internet Explorer) can immediately display a rough image after just a little bit of it has been downloaded, and then sketch in the details as they come in. Figure 8.2 shows an early glimpse at a GIF in the process of downloading to a browser.

In Chapter 9 we'll discuss one more trick with GIFs: animation.

Pros and Cons of JPEGs

JPEG is the superior format for photographs, as its standard was arrived at for that specific purpose. JPEGs can store up to millions of colors. When creating a JPEG (saving a file or converting it from another format), you can choose a degree of compression, keeping in mind that greater compression means greater loss of the original image data.

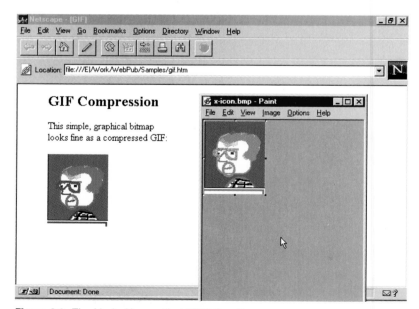

Figure 8.1 The kind of image that "GIFs" well

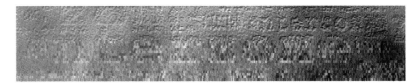

Figure 8.2 Interlaced GIFs look interesting faster

For best photographic reproduction, take slides and use a slide scanner instead of scanning prints with a traditional flat-bed scanner. Any good service bureau or desktop publishing shop should have a slide scanner.

Since your art will eventually appear on the Web in 72 dots-per-inch resolution, you don't need to scan it at incredibly high resolution. 100 dots per inch should be fine for photographic images. For graphic art, scan as close to the resolution as the art was created with (it depends on the printer).

Figure 8.3 shows the same photograph with three different levels of JPEG compression.

CREATING GRAPHICS

There are two ways to create art for your Web page. You can "draw" it, using a drafting and art program, creating it from scratch with the computer. Or you can scan existing photography or line art, and either manipulate it to your specific needs, or just reproduce it as close to the original as possible.

Professional graphic designers can usually give you electronic files in the format you request (or in a format you can convert to GIF or

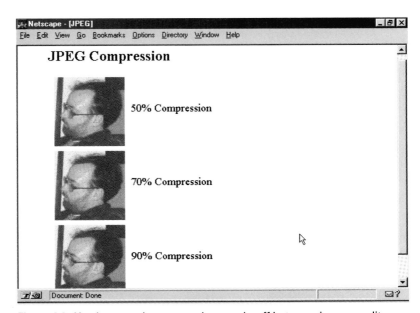

Figure 8.3 You have to choose your best trade-off between image quality and download speed. (This is what we mean when we talk about limitations of bandwidth)

JPEG). Existing camera-ready art, such as letterhead, can always be scanned.

Figure 8.4 shows scanner software with a series of scanned images for an artist's gallery installation.

Most scanner software creates TIFF images. TIFFs can be converted to JPEGs or GIFs with most common graphics software packages. (See "Converting Existing Graphics," coming up.)

OBTAINING GRAPHICS

There are many ways to find graphics if you can't create (or commission) your own. Old-fashioned clip art, which used to appear in large books for cut-and-paste insertion into newspaper pages, can now be purchased as graphic images on a CD-ROM. There are images on the Net that are both free for download and free to use. There are images that can be used for non-commercial purposes only, or with the permission of the artist, and there are images that may not be reused for any purposes.

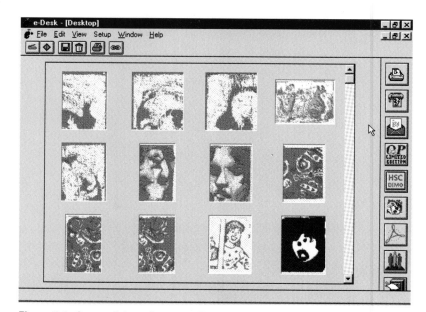

Figure 8.4 Some of these images will appear at the Iconica gallery (**http://ezone.org:1080/icon/**)

Photoshop is also responsible for the most common graphical elements seen on the Web—everything from shiny, embossed, and beveled clickable buttons, to little floating candy bullets.

habits & strategies

When converting an image, don't save it with more colors than the image actually requires, or you'll be forcing the file to be much larger with no benefit. For good advice on choosing colors that will look good on all platforms, see The Browser Safe Color Palette (http://www.lynda.com/hex.html), an excellent discussion with samples.

CONVERTING EXISTING GRAPHICS

Most of the time, you'll need to convert your graphics to GIF or JPEG format. Some scanner software can produce one or both of these formats automatically. If you have a program that can convert between GIFs and JPEGs, then you just need to be able to get existing images into one of those formats to have both options.

There are a variety of programs used for various aspects of Web production. Sometimes a simple tool for cropping or converting is easier to use than a system-intensive program such as Photoshop (which, incidentally, now comes with a GIF plug-in, and can therefore save images in both JPEG and GIF formats).

On the high end, Photoshop has been the industry standard for ages, used for creating logos, editing and processing images, effects, and so on. There are other programs that do similar things—notably Paint Shop Pro, an inexpensive shareware alternative—but Photoshop seems to be the tool of choice for high-end image production work. Figure 8.5 shows a scanned TIFF image being saved as a JPEG graphic in Photoshop.

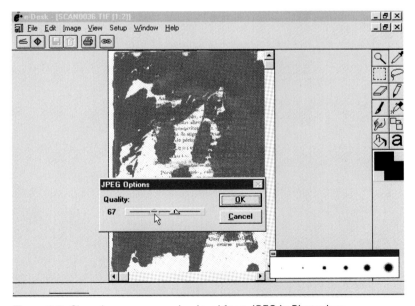

Figure 8.5 Choosing a compression level for a JPEG in Photoshop

You may, when converting images, also decide to perform some simple editing on them, such as recropping to focus on one part of the image. Most image-processing software, ranging from shareware, like Lview Pro, to professional commercial software, like Photoshop, can handle cropping and resizing images.

When converting, you may sometimes have to change a file into a more common intermediate format (such as TIFF or BMP on the PC, or PICT on the Mac).

INSERTING GRAPHICS INTO PAGES

Once you have your graphics prepared for the Web, inserting them into your pages is a breeze with Netscape Editor. When you insert your graphics, you can specify all the formatting controls you want to apply, or you can insert them and then change their formatting at any time in the future.

Formatting Graphics While Inserting Them

Before inserting a graphic, place the insertion point where you want it to appear. The easiest way to insert a graphic into your document is to click the Insert Image button.

If you haven't saved your document yet, Netscape Editor will prompt you to do so.

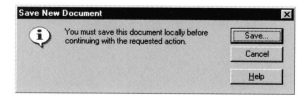

When linking to graphics, be sure to warn your readers of any large file sizes (say anything above 50K), as mentioned in Chapter 7.

Click save and save the document. The Properties dialog box will appear (see Figure 8.6).

Type the path and file name of the image, if you know it, or click the Browse button to the right of the Image file name box. Find the file you want in the Select Image File dialog box and then click the Open button.

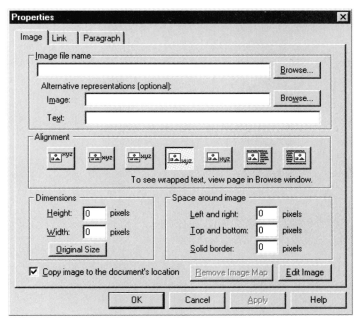

Figure 8.6 The Properties dialog box for images makes it easy to control the appearance of art as you insert it

Low-Resolution Alternative Image

If you want a low-resolution alternative image to display first to give your reader something to look at before the real art arrives, press TAB and type the path and file name of the other image file, or click the Browse button. Find the file you want in the Select Low Resolution Image dialog box and then click the Open button.

Here's a low-resolution graphic being updated by a higher-resolution image:

habits & strategies

Always type some alternative text. Text-only browsers will display [IMAGE] in the place of any image if you leave out alternative text. Either identify the image or give substitute information.

Alternative Text

Next press TAB and type some alternative text to explain the image to those who can't see it (or type " " if you want nothing to display in place of the image).

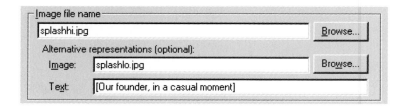

Figure 8.7 shows a Web page with image-loading turned off and alternative text showing in the place of images.

To make it possible for text-only browsers to download an image file, you have to make it into a link to itself. For more on this, see the section called "Making a Graphic into a Link," coming up.

Alignment

Now it's time to decide how you want the image to fit in with the text on the page. Most of the time you'll want text to appear below the image or alongside it. Netscape Editor offers all the standard alignment choices, presenting them in the form of pictorial buttons that demonstrate how the text will wrap around the graphic.

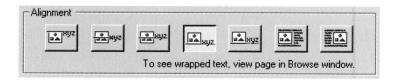

CAUTION

As of version 3.0, Netscape Editor won't display text wrapped around graphics. You'll have to preview your page in Browser View to see that effect.

habits & strategies

If you're not sure of the height and width of your image, view it directly in Netscape Navigator (using the File | Open File in Browser command) and you'll see the dimensions spelled out in Navigator's title bar.

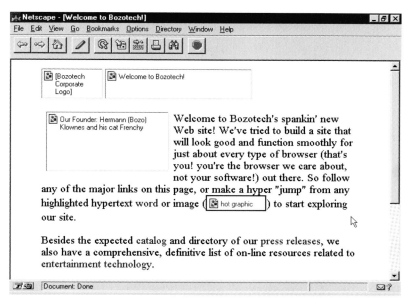

Figure 8.7 Alt text: it's de rigeur.

If you want text to appear next to your graphic, you'll want to put in some horizontal spacing to create a gutter (or, more loosely, some "breathing room") around the picture. How you'll do that is coming up.

Specifying Height and Width

Any time you specify an image's height and width in your document, you help it load faster in a browser. The browser can leave the right amount of space for the picture and keep laying out the page (namely, the text that has to flow around the images), without waiting for the image to arrive before continuing. For visual effects, you can also distort the appearance of an image by deliberately entering height and width information that differs from the image's actual dimensions.

Although it's not universally supported yet and Netscape Editor doesn't help you do it, it's also possible to specify the dimensions of an image in terms of a percentage of the screen height or width. This should only be used with special art that will look good with varying proportions.

To use the actual dimensions of the image, you can just leave the boxes set to zero (0) the first time you insert a graphic. Later, if you come back and edit it, the actual measurements will appear in those boxes.

Spacing Around an Image

If you want a little padding between an image and surrounding text (or the next image over), you can specify a number of pixels of blank space for either the left and right sides or the top and bottom sides (horizontal and vertical spacing, respectively). You cannot (yet) put different amounts of spacing on, say, the left and right sides.

You can also specify an amount of additional padding surrounding the entire image, called the border. The border puts a uniform amount of spacing on all four sides of the image. Normally invisible, a border will appear with link coloring if the image is used as a hyperlink. You can set the border to zero (0) to hide this hyperlink giveaway (if you believe it mars the appearance of the page, for example) in Browser View. However, in Netscape Editor, the border will appear no matter what, to remind you that the image is a link.

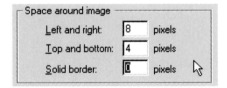

Where to Put the Image?

There are two different methods you can use for storing your images. The easiest method is to keep all images used on a given page within the same folder (or directory) as the page itself. This works best unless you have certain images that are used in many different pages. If you do, then it does not make sense to keep a separate copy of such an image in every folder where it might appear.

By default, an option called Copy image to the document's location is checked to bring any image you insert onto the page into the same folder as the document. Uncheck it if you have already placed the image in a different folder, as long as it retains the same relative relationship to the current folder that it will have when published on the server.

Editing Graphics on the Fly

If you plan to actually work on or change an image while inserting it, click the Edit Image button. If you've never established a program as your default image editor, Netscape Editor will prompt you to do so.

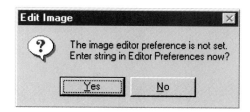

Click Yes and then TAB down to the Image box in the Editor Preferences dialog box that appears. Type the path and file name of your image-editing program or click the Browse button, find the program, and then click Open.

Netscape Editor will launch your image editor. Edit the file, save it, and quit the launched program when you're done. You'll be back in the dialog box in Netscape Editor.

trends

HTML 3.2 promotes a new image tag to replace the <IMG SRC="filename"> used for all in-line images up to now. The <FIG> tag would still have a SRC="filename" component, but it would also have a closing </FIG> tag (the IMG tag stands alone) and it could then surround formatted alternative text.

Another way of using graphics to link to other pages is via clickable image maps. See Chapter 12 for more on how to create them.

Making a Graphic into a Link

If you want the graphic you're inserting to function as a link the same way the text links (described in Chapter 7) do, then click the Link tab on the Properties dialog box (see Figure 8.8).

Type a page location (for an external document) or click the Browse button to choose a document from your local site-in-development.

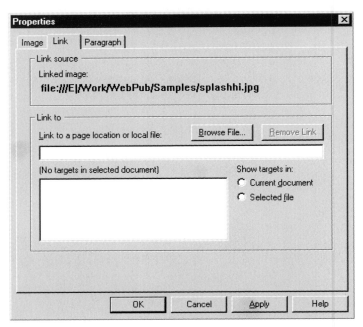

Figure 8.8 The Link tab for image properties is nearly identical to that for text properties

One way to give your readers an informed choice about whether to download large art files is to present them with "thumbnail" versions of the linked art. A thumbnail is a much smaller, often heavily compressed, version of a graphic, displayed on the linking page.

When linking *to* a large graphic, be sure to warn your readers of the large file size so they can decide ahead of time whether to download the page.

Actually Inserting the Image

When you're done choosing all the options for your image, click OK. The image will be inserted into your document (see Figure 8.9).

Dragging Graphics onto Pages

There's one other way of inserting images into a Web document, which is especially convenient if you have a bunch of art files in the

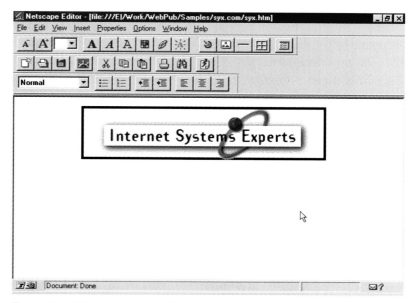

Figure 8.9 A Web document with an image inserted

same folder and you need to insert them onto a page, or a series of pages. Netscape Editor enables you to simply drag an image icon into the editing area of a document to insert the image. This is called drag and drop.

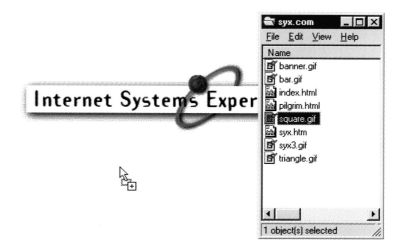

Once you've inserted the image, you can select it and change its properties if you need to fine-tune it.

Changing How Graphics Are Displayed

Once you've got an image inserted into your document, it can be moved around just as you move text around in the flow of paragraphs. You can select an image, cut it, and paste it elsewhere.

If you want to change any of the display features (such as the alignment of the figure, its size, the spacing around it, alternative text, and so on), just right-click on the image (click and hold with a Mac) and then select Image Properties from the menu that pops up.

Or select Properties I Images. This brings up the Properties dialog box described in the previous few sections.

I Break for Images

To control the way images and text stack up, you might sometimes want to insert a break after an image. To do this, select Insert I Break Below Image(s).

CONTROLLING THE LOOK OF THE PAGE

In the beginning, the Web consisted of just black text (and downloadable files). Graphical browsers introduced inline artwork but generally, Web pages still featured black text on a gunmetal gray background. Version 1.1 of Netscape Navigator introduced a new feature (that was already in the works for the HTML 3 specification)—custom text and background colors, and the ability to use graphical "wallpaper" files as background art (the image is "tiled"—repeated across and down to fill the available space).

If you don't specify any of these features, then Netscape browsers will display pages with black text on a white or gray background. Links will be blue before they've been clicked, red while being clicked, and purple after they've been clicked. Any user can, of course, customize their own browser and choose any color scheme they want, but very few users do this. Most accept the default color scheme and thereby any color scheme imposed on pages by their designers.

If you've tried out Netscape's Page Wizard, then you've already seen how graphics can be used as background tiles.

By the way, the Netscape commands that control the look of the page are inserted into the BODY tag.

CAUTION

Pages consisting of white text on a dark background may not be printable if the browser tries to print white text on white paper.

habits & strategies

One way to unify the design of your Web site is to choose a color scheme that matches the colors in your logo or your other graphical design elements.

Some Basic Design Principles

Just because you *can* play around with the color scheme, it doesn't mean you *should*. It just means you should consider it as one of your design options. For text-oriented pages, you should make sure primarily that your readers will be comfortable reading the words. There should be a sharp contrast between the text and background colors. It's very popular these days to have white or yellow text on black or dark blue backgrounds, to get that space-age effect. However, that sort of presentation, while dramatic, can be difficult on the eyes if you have to read a lot of it (see Figure 8.10).

Stick generally to dark text colors and pale, muted background colors. If you plan to use a graphical image as a background, you'll likewise be better off with a pale or faint image, rather than one which will compete visually with the overlying text.

The Netscape commands that control the look of the page are not standard HTML 2.0 (they were adopted in HTML 3.2), but more and more competing browsers are incorporating these features. Make sure your design will work just as well, however, for people who don't get the benefit of your tasteful color selections. And don't refer to your color scheme in the text. Don't write, "Click any chartreuse-colored words to follow a link," or anything like that. (This is a corollary to the rule against writing "Click here!" anywhere on your pages.)

With all our advice and cautions aside, don't be intimidated about taking advantage of the color options. Used well, color selections can add a high level of "gloss" or slickness to your site design.

Choosing Colors for a Page

Netscape Editor offers you two ways of customizing the color scheme of a Web page. You can choose from one of its predefined color schemes, or you can select specific colors for each of the five elements you can customize (text, links, visited links, active links, and background).

No matter which method you plan to use, you start by selecting Properties I Document. This brings up the Document Properties dialog box. Click the Appearance tab.

habits & strategies

Even if you prefer Netscape's default color scheme, you can select it in the Color schemes box so that other browsers, no matter what their default schemes are, will display your pages the way Netscape displays them.

Figure 8.10 You'll see lots of Web sites with this sort of color scheme, but it's kinda tough on the eyes

For a new, blank document, Use Browser's colors will be selected by default, meaning the document will be displayed with whatever preferred or default color scheme each user's browser has in place. For most people, that will mean the default Netscape color scheme we discussed previously. To select custom color options, click Use custom colors.

Using a Predefined Color Scheme

If you don't wish to consider every possible combination of colors, you may find one of Netscape's predefined color schemes to your liking. To consider a scheme, click the drop-down list-box in the Color schemes area near the top of the Document Properties dialog box.

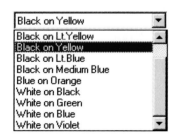

A scrollable menu will drop down. Use your arrow keys to move through the list. As each new color scheme is selected, the examples in the custom colors area below change to reflect the selected scheme, as shown here.

If you find a color scheme you like, click OK. If not, try choosing custom colors for each of the design elements.

Think about the possible

hardware limitations of your

audience. Most Macintosh

users, for example, can see a

huge variety of colors, but many

Windows users still live in a

256-color universe. It's a good

idea to avoid colors that look

polka-dotty on lower-resolution

screens (such as the back-

ground of the Black on

Off-White scheme).

Selecting Text Colors

You follow a single procedure repeatedly to choose colors for each of the text types. To select a basic color for non-hyperlink text, click the Normal Text button in the Custom colors area.

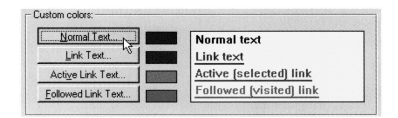

This brings up the Color dialog box. It offers a basic palette of 48 colors (with 16 slots for custom colors, which we'll get to later). To choose any of the colors, just click on its swatch.

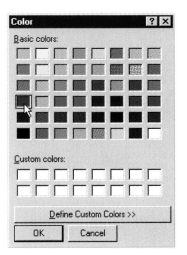

Then click OK. Repeat the process for each of the text elements. Every time you choose a color, it will change the overall look of your custom color scheme, so you may find yourself backtracking and second-guessing some of your choices until you find an arrangement you like.

Background Colors

The process for selecting a background color is about the same as for text colors. Just click the Choose Color button in the Background area.

This brings up the same Color dialog box shown in the previous illustration. Choose a background color and click OK.

Defining Your Own Colors

If you're not satisfied with any of the 48 colors offered for either text or background, you can try to zero in on the exact color you want using the custom color picker. First you have to click the appropriate button for the element you plan to change (for example, Normal text) and bring up the Color dialog box. Then click the Define Custom Colors >> button. This will expand the Color dialog box to include a graphical color chart (see Figure 8.11).

The square area plots hue (what most people call color, as in red, green, blue, etc.) versus saturation (which you can think of as how bright or dull the color is). The vertical bar next to it allows you to choose luminosity (which is the amount of lightness or darkness in the color). But you don't have to think in such quasi-scientific terms. Really, you just click in the square to get roughly the right color you want, and then click in the bar to fine tune it. And, as with most things, you'll probably have to go back and forth a little to get it right.

If you're mathematically inclined, you can try entering hue, saturation, and luminosity values directly into the text boxes provided—or you can enter values for red, green, and blue (another way of defining colors on the computer)—all in a range from 0 to 255.

When (and if) you find a color you like, click the Add to Custom Colors button to add it to one of the blank swatches in the Custom colors area in the bottom-left of the dialog box. This new color will now be part of your palette and can be selected for any of the colored elements.

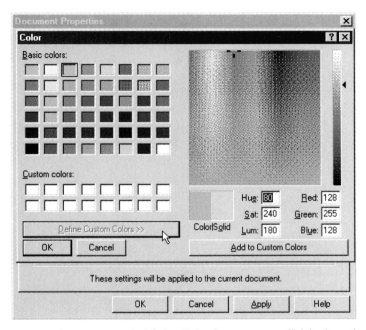

Figure 8.11 With the expanded Color dialog box, you can click in the color square to select a hue and saturation and then click in the vertical bar to choose a luminosity; or you can type in exact numbers for the color you want

Background Patterns on Pages

If you have an image you want to use as a background tile, insert its path and file name here in the Background section of the Document Properties dialog box. Not every image can work as a tile, because the edges have to fit together without looking awkward or jarring. If you're interested in trying to make your own background tiles, you might want to pick up the plug-in package for Photoshop called Kai's Power Tools. Its "texturizer" module is designed to turn graphic images into wallpaper tiles.

You can find tiles for free on the Internet, although you can't necessarily use them for commercial purposes without permission or without paying for them. You can also buy CD-ROMs full of background tiles and other stock images.

You can create a parchment effect for your backdrop by scanning a piece of slightly rough or off-white paper and cropping the scan down to a small non-descript portion, such as the image shown here:

Another useful background trick is to create a long, narrow, two-tone tile and use it to create a strip of color across the top or left side of the page. For example, this graphic,

when used as a tile, will create a page background like the one shown in Figure 8.12.

CAUTION

It gets harder to lay out a page when you're forced to keep some of the text in one area (for example, over a strip of color), especially when you can't be sure of the exact font settings your readers might be using. The best you can do, usually, is make a design that looks acceptable for most people.

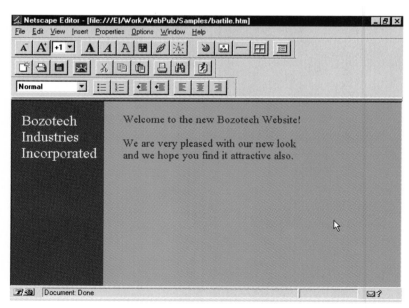

Figure 8.12 This page uses a two-tone tile to create the colored area

A new way to create different colored areas on a page is by establishing different background colors for each cell in a table. (Tables are explained in Chapter 10.)

Done Sprucing Up Your Page?

Once you've made all your color and image selections, click the OK button.

WHAT'S NEXT?

Chapter 9 will show you how to incorporate other forms of media, ranging from sounds to video clips, to produce full-fledged multimedia presentations at your Web site.

9

Creating a Multimedia Feast for the Senses

FAST FORWARD

BE THOUGHTFUL TO YOUR AUDIENCE ➤ *p. 182-190*

- Figure out a maximum practical file size for downloads and stick to it.
- Warn your audience when a link connects to a large file (anything over 50K or so).
- Use extra media elements only when they serve a definite purpose.

INSERT A LINK TO A MULTIMEDIA OBJECT ➤ *p. 191*

1. Click the Make Link button.
2. Choose the file name (or URL) of the object.
3. Click OK.

INSERT AN IMAGE-TYPE ANIMATION ➤ *pp. 191-192*

1. Click the Insert Image button.
2. Choose the file name (or URL) of the animation.
3. Click OK.

Back in the '70s when we used the term *multimedia,* it meant slide shows with narration and possibly music or video. Today, the term almost always refers to computer presentations that make use of more than one medium. Beyond text, this usually means images, sounds, animations, video, and even three-dimensional, virtual-reality environments. Loosely, the term is used for any form of computer data that offers some presentation or entertainment value.

We could obviously fill an entire book with techniques for developing and integrating multimedia content, but you're too busy for that level of detail. Instead, we'll give you an overview of the formats that exist for the various media and how to integrate these formats into your Web documents. As with most of the more "advanced" topics in this book, if you have elaborate ambitions about bells and whistles in your Web site, then you'll probably be happiest hiring a professional to pull it off for you.

The Web was invented as a vehicle for exchanging files of many sorts. Then the graphical paradigm took over from the text-based roots of collaborative communication that the Web was founded on. We're in the midst of another such migration towards "plugging in" output from high-end authoring tools into Web presentations. Traditionally (in the last few years, that is!), HTML has restricted designers from creating a true What-You-See-Is-What-You-Get package and has allowed users to customize fonts, colors, and different browsers to interpret the same pages in different ways. From a design standpoint, this is sheer hell! One can never be sure what the end user will see. So it's not surprising that the addition of inline Acrobat, Director, and QuickTime files into Web pages has been the big promise of the Web since 1995. Netscape comes automatically installed with Shockwave, an inline Director viewer application, so this is one of the most popular multimedia plug-ins currently around. The ability to offer consistent packaging of what the user sees is likely to become increasingly

habits & strategies

Consider farming out the things you can't do well yourself, especially while you're learning. There's too much to the Web to just be a good enough generalist.

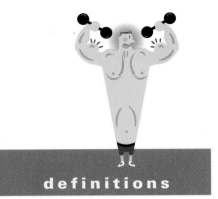

kbps: *Kilobits per second, a measurement of bandwidth (the number of bits that can be sent through a medium divided by a unit of time). A kilobit is 1024 bits.*

Mbps: *Megabits per second, a larger measurement of bandwidth. A megabit is 1,048,576 bits.*

important as the wars between corporate "enhancements" to become the next Web standards continue to drive the market.

So there's a mad rush to dump QuickTime and Director movies or any sort of multimedia besides plain text and graphics (and sound, which we'll get to later) onto the Web. As with graphics, there's a tendency to underestimate the time and skill that goes into creating good multimedia presentations or good audio productions. It's the sort of thing that many people think they can just go out and buy a piece of software for.

THINK AGAIN: WHO'S YOUR AUDIENCE?

It's a good idea to consider your audience before you rush into dumping multimedia on the Web. Most multimedia applications create large files—huge by modem transmission-time standards. Transmission speeds vary. You may find yourself targeting an internal audience via ethernet (on your intranet, that is) that can handle the bandwidth needed, or an external audience that might include few who are able, practically speaking, to spend the time downloading a file larger than one megabyte. Or you might have to serve both types of audiences equally.

What looks great on your local server may crawl over a 14.4 kbps modem. If you use other distribution mediums, such as including multimedia presentations on a floppy disk or CD-ROM, those might be a better way to reach your audience.

Table 9.1 provides a more detailed comparison of download times for different bandwidths and typical file sizes. Note that these are *optimal* download times and actual times can be even longer! (Also, all the amounts are approximate and rounded off, anyway.)

POPULAR MULTIMEDIA FORMATS

Although the list of file formats that can be served up over the Web is growing all the time, there are several major categories of multimedia objects, and in each of those categories there are some

	Slow Modem (14.4 kbps)	Fast Modem (28.8 kbps)	ISDN / Frame Relay (64 kbps)	T1 (1.544Mbps)	T3 (44.736 Mbps)
Small HTML or Text file (4K)	2+ seconds	1+ seconds	.5 second	.02 second	.0007 second
400 x 500 compressed JPEG image (15K)	8+ seconds	4+ seconds	2 seconds	.08 second	.003 second
30-page PDF file (100K)	1 minute	.5 minute	10 seconds	.5 second	.02 second
4-second sound clip (900K)	8+ minutes	4+ minutes	2- minutes	4.5 seconds	.16 second
Software (5M)	1+ hours	.5 hour	11 minutes	30 seconds	1 second

Table 9.1 Comparing Download Times for Different Sized Files and Level of Connection

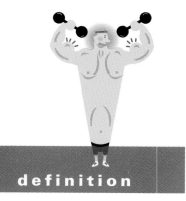

definition

inline: *Appearing in the midst of a Web document, instead of in a separate window (a term from traditional publishing).*

dominant applications and file formats you should know about. We'll quickly run through them in this section.

Bear in mind that most of these multimedia objects will not be displayed "inline" (on the Web document page) by most Web browsers. Some browsers will launch external "helper applications," when available, to run and display linked files. With the appropriate viewers "plugged in," others can display such objects inline. Currently, Netscape Navigator features the widest set of third-party plug-in products that can be used alongside the browser.

bookmark

*For more on plug-ins currently designed for Netscape, go to Netscape's plug-in page (currently at **http://home.netscape.com/comprod/mirror/navcomponents_download.html**) or to BrowserWatch's Plug-in Plaza (at **http://www.browserwatch.com/**).*

Most of the time you can't assume that your readers have the necessary viewer (or playback) software or plug-ins. To deal with this uncertainty, you can include links from your pages (or from a centralized "resource" page) to Web sites where your audience can go to down-

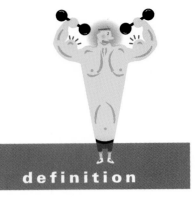

PDF: *Adobe's portable document format, a page-description file format that permits a high level of formatting and layout control while keeping the ultimate size of the files relatively small. PDF files can also contain hyperlinks.*

load the extra tools they need. Bear in mind, however, that many readers will simply forego the extra steps necessary and miss out on the extra content.

Formatted Documents (Adobe Acrobat)

Adobe was quick to see the rise of the Web and HTML as a free standard and they released the Adobe Acrobat reader as a free Web helper application before Netscape even had a product out. The inline display of Acrobat files in Netscape Navigator (using Adobe's Acrobat 3.0 plug-in) has been available for a short while. Acrobat's PDF file offers a true WYSIWYG format for designers to ensure that the reader sees the text and layout exactly as desired.

For existing print matter, the cost of developing Acrobat files is far lower than HTML. Acrobat also makes it easier to preserve a consistent print look and feel in an electronic format. Until recently, HTML couldn't even put columns of text side by side. Acrobat files can't be dissected or edited with the ease that HTML can be copied. For these reasons, the IRS uses Acrobat to distribute online tax forms (at **http://www.irs.ustreas.gov**), as shown in Figure 9-1, and the *New York Times* uses it to post the TimesFAX version of the newspaper to the Web (at **http://www.nytimesfax.com**).

bookmark

*Get your IRS tax forms at **http://www.irs.ustreas.gov**. See TimesFax at **http://www.nytimesfax.com**.*

The New York Times *quickly realized that they were limiting their audience too severely with only a PDF version of the newspaper on the Web, so they now produce* CyberTimes, *at **http://www.nytimes.com** or Killersites' PDF page (**http://www.killersite.com/3-PDF**).*

Making PDF files requires a driver called the PDFwriter, which enables your usual programs (anything from Word to QuarkXpress) to save files in this format. PDF files are often relatively large (compared to HTML files) and can take a while to display. Mechanisms to page forward or read pages while a file is downloading have recently been

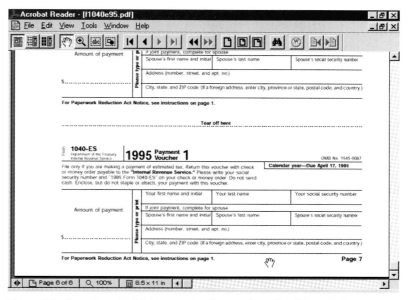

Figure 9.1 A tax form in Adobe Acrobat format, from the IRS web site

implemented, but whoever maintains your server for you will need to take care of this. (See Chapter 13 for more on servers). As much as possible, design PDF files in ways that minimize file size.

habits & strategies

Break large files into smaller sections or chapters if possible to speed up network access to subsections.

bookmark

For more information about Adobe Acrobat and the PDF format, visit ***http://www.adobe.com*** *or* ***http://www.projectcool.com/developer/acrobat.***

Sounds (WAV, ULAW, AIFF, and Real Audio)

Right now, there is no single sound format that you can expect all users to be able to hear. The Sun ULAW (.au) format was the first popular Web sound format, but in recent years it has been largely eclipsed by Microsoft's WAV and Macintosh's AIFF formats. Fortunately, there are many sound utility programs out there that can convert

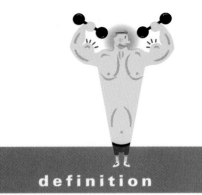

from one format to another. Your best bet, usually, is to make your sound files available in more than one format, so that your readers can decide for themselves which format to choose.

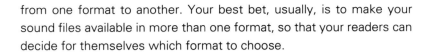

(best heard read aloud [.wav (690 k), AIFF (527 k)])

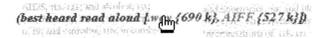

definition

streaming: *A sound or other media format is said to be streaming if the playback mechanism can start playing it before the entire file has been downloaded.*

Traditionally, large media files such as sounds or movies have had to be downloaded completely before you can see or hear anything at all. The latest development in sound reproduction over the Web is *streaming* sound. The most widespread format for streaming sound is Progressive Networks' RealAudio. One drawback to RealAudio is that you need to purchase a special RealAudio server from Progressive to be able to "serve" your own sounds, although you can produce the sounds themselves (that is, convert sounds from one of the static formats to RealAudio's streaming format) with free software from Progressive Networks. The sound quality is still below the level of a radio (it's monophonic, for example), and there are drop-outs from time to time, but if you have a lot of sound data to send over the Net, it's the only practical solution these days.

bookmark

*RealAudio is at **http://www.realaudio.com.***

Microsoft also has introduced a BGSOUND tag to go inside the BODY tag and define a background sound that plays automatically when you visit a page, but so far only Microsoft Internet Explorer recognizes that tag.

Netscape Navigator is distributed with its own, minimal LiveAudio (non-streaming) sound player software, but you can download the RealAudio helper program from **http://www.realaudio.com**. Figure 9-2 shows the RealAudio playback box that pops up when a reader selects a RealAudio sound for listening.

Microsoft has promoted a rival streaming sound format called TrueSpeech from the DSP Group (**http://www.dspg.com**). It is not as well established, but it's an alternative you might want to consider. Netscape has licensed another rival streaming sound format, call VOXware, which you can read up on at the Netscape site.

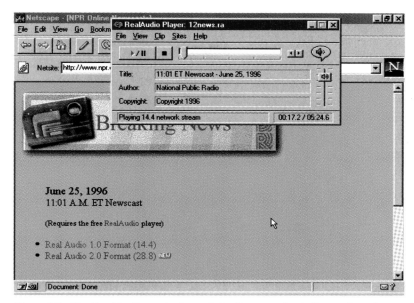

Figure 9.2 The RealAudio control panel, for listeners, is similar to the primary controls of a tape deck or VCR

Movies and Animations (QuickTime, MPEG, AVI, and GIF89a)

Although the terms "movie," "video," and "animation" are often used more or less interchangeably, they do denote slightly different things. Any sort of moving image file can be called a movie. Photographic moving images are usually referred to as video. Animation suggests any kind of drawn or otherwise rendered images, likewise moving. The common denominator is movement. Traditionally, there are a number of competing high-end movie formats (high-end for computers, still at the low- to medium-end when compared to television reproduction): an international standard movie format called MPEG (which stands for Motion Picture Experts Group), Microsoft's AVI format, something called VDOlive, and the Macintosh QuickTime format. All of these formats involve some degree of compression and all of them existed before the popular explosion of the Web.

As with other multimedia formats, some browsers can launch external playback applications and some can handle plug-ins to produce inline movies. Just this year, an inline QuickTime plug-in for Netscape Navigator arrived on the scene, for example.

In the fertile laboratory of the online world, new innovative ways of distributing movies have come about, mostly on the animation side of things. Netscape introduced so-called "server push" (or CGI) animations, a simple type of script with which a series of still images can be repeatedly sent to the same image space on a Web page to create a movie-like effect—something like a child's flipcard animation compared to other formats of computer animation of art or video. A big drawback: CGI animations can rarely reach the 12 frames a second speed required for the human eye to see motion.

The latest innovation sweeping the Web these days is GIF89a animation. GIF89a is an update of the GIF format (yes, the one agreed upon back in 1989) that permits a GIF file to contain a series of still images and commands for things such as looping and delays between the appearance of each frame. This turns out to be a very quick-and-dirty way of putting together simple animations. Many of the popular image processing software packages (such as Adobe PhotoShop) have recently made GIF89a plug-ins available to facilitate development of these animations. There are also excellent shareware tools available for Windows and Macintosh. Because many browsers (including pre-2.0 versions of Netscape) do not fully implement the GIF89a standard, some viewers will see only the first frame of such an animation. Make sure that first frame is a suitable still illustration for your page! If you looked at Netscape's Page Wizard (discussed in Chapter 4) then you may remember the animated bullets you could choose. Those were GIF animations.

For more on server push and other CGI-script tricks, see Chapter 12.

bookmark

*To create your own GIF animations in Windows, download the GIF Construction Set (**http://www.mindworkshop.com/alchemy/alchemy.html**). On the Mac side, try GifBuilder (**http://www.pascal.com/mirrors/gifbuilder**). For more information, see Royal Frazier's definitive Web site on the subject (**http://member.aol.com/royalef/gifanim.htm**).*

The biggest obstacle to using a movie in your pages is that almost all formats require a file to download 100% before the user can see it played on an external viewer. They aren't integrated into the pages and they change the experience of browsing Web pages. They are also typically huge in file size. By the time your users finish downloading the whole file they might be off at some other Web site on the other side of the world! That is, *if* they download the whole file and actually view it!

trends

An alternative to GIF animation that requires a special plug-in but is faster, more compact, and streaming, is FutureWave's Cell Animator (and FutureSplash plug-in), available from **http://www.futurewave.com.** *(See* **http://www.sos.net/home/jef/test/fff1.htm** *for examples of animations created with these tools.)*

Other types of video formats that make use of streaming include Xing's StreamWorks, InterVU, VDOlive, Cool Fusion, Vosaic, Vivo, and plug-ins for QuickTime and the Microsoft AVI format. Expect to see more of the bulky media formats evolve into streaming variants to make the browsing experience more coherent.

Popular tools for creating animations include Cell Animator and Sizzler. Technically, Java can be used to create animations, but that wouldn't be a very efficient way to go about doing it.

Interactive Multimedia Objects

Another type of "medium" that can be inserted into Web documents is that of interactive applications or applets. Traditionally, such self-running small applications could be created with such tools as MacroMedia Director. Director allows for the integration of multiple media, such as images, movies, and sounds, along with user-controls such as buttons and "hot" clickable areas. As mentioned earlier, Netscape can display Director files inline with its built-in Shockwave reader.

189

Another interim solution, currently geared toward the Microsoft ActiveX standard, is a plug-in called mBED. It extends HTML to include a number of commands that can be used to control animations and other multimedia events.

Meanwhile, the direction for development of online applications is moving toward the Java and JavaScript standards promoted by a consortium of prominent computer companies (minus Microsoft) on the one hand, and the ActiveX and Visual Basic Script standard promoted by Microsoft to blend together its OLE (Object Linking and Embedding) system used in Windows with the Web. These various scripting formats all make it possible to control the playback or response of multimedia objects. See Chapter 12 for more on applets and scripting on the Web.

Three-Dimensional Environments (VRML)

It is already possible to author three-dimensional environments (virtual reality) and make them viewable and browsable via the Web. This requires either specialized Web browsers, helper applications, or inline plug-ins. So far, Netscape has the largest number of inline VRML (Virtual Reality Modeling Language) plug-ins already available. (Internet Explorer also has a VRML plug-in.) The challenge, of course, is in developing fully detailed and responsive three-dimensional spaces. As with other sophisticated file formats, VRML files can be huge and take prohibitively long to download over modems.

MULTIMEDIA FOR INTRANETS

Most of the bandwidth limitations you have to consider when developing multimedia content for the Internet can be much less of an issue if the content need only be distributed over a local intranet (a local-area network set up with Internet protocols which is capable of supporting standard Internet tools, such as Web browsers and plug-ins). For such in-house demonstrations and applications such as training, briefings, and orientations, the Web might be the easiest way to assemble the multimedia components. If you need such a presentation to be more portable, you can still keep it on a diskette and then show it to your audience on a local PC or network. For that matter, if you have enough large material, it might justify pressing a CD-ROM of the content for easy distribution.

INSERTING MULTIMEDIA OBJECTS

Multimedia objects can either be connected to a primary Web page by means of hyperlinks or directly embedded. Some objects, such as GIF or server-push animations, use graphics formats and can be inserted directly as images. Others must be embedded with the <EMBED> tag.

habits & strategies

You are not limited to linking to or embedding objects located on your local machine or site. Because of the flexibility of URLs (see Chapter 7 for more on them), you can link to any object located on a public Internet server. (Get permission first, if you did not create the object.)

trends

HTML 3.2 points the way towards a generalized OBJECT tag that will be used to insert any type of medium directly into a web page, embedding it inline. So far, though, this standard has not been implemented.

As explained in Chapter 7, you insert a hyperlink by clicking the Make Link button.

Then, in the dialog box that appears, you can name the linked document and choose the "multimedia" file you want to make available to your audience.

For objects that can be treated as images, as explained in Chapter 8, insert them with the Insert Image button.

You'll also have to make sure that the server your site is on knows how to serve up the multimedia file formats you're using. See Chapter 13 for more on server issues.

Then, in the dialog box that appears, name the GIF animation or CGI script or other object that functions like an image.

Remember to include a warning, such as (125K), with links to large objects, so people with slow connections know what they're getting into. Also, include links to download locations for any plug-ins or special helper applications your objects might require.

To embed an object, you have to enter HTML directly into your document, since Netscape Editor, so far, does not support the <EMBED> tag. EMBED resembles both the anchor tag and the image tag, somewhat. A typical embedded file might be coded like this:

```
<EMBED SRC="movie.avi">
```

Optionally, you can specify the height and/or width of the inline object, either as a precise number of pixels or as percentages of the window (or table) height and width, like so:

```
<EMBED SRC="movie.avi" HEIGHT=150 WIDTH=400>
```

See Chapter 11 for how to insert your own tags directly.

MULTIMEDIA ADVICE IN A NUTSHELL

Finally, the best advice we can offer is to design for today's needs. Break up big presentations into smaller ones. Consider your audience and if there's a better way of serving them high-bandwidth multimedia. What works for a CD-ROM might very well not work on the Web. Keep in mind that the Web is best suited for fast-changing data and quick design and implementation. (It's more of a "live" medium than a "recorded" medium.) Things get dated fast if they try to be state of the art. Small, elegant, sparse—keep it simple and get the point across. Don't lean on multimedia as a substitute for content. Be careful about trying to repackage video, PowerPoint slides, or other existing creations into a Web pipeline. Half-hour infomercials and home videos probably are better off in the context they were created for!

WHAT'S NEXT?

Chapter 10 shows you how to create tables and how to use them to produce more sophisticated looking HTML layouts. Chapter 11 shows you how to insert features that even Netscape Editor does not know how to do into your Web documents.

CHAPTER 10

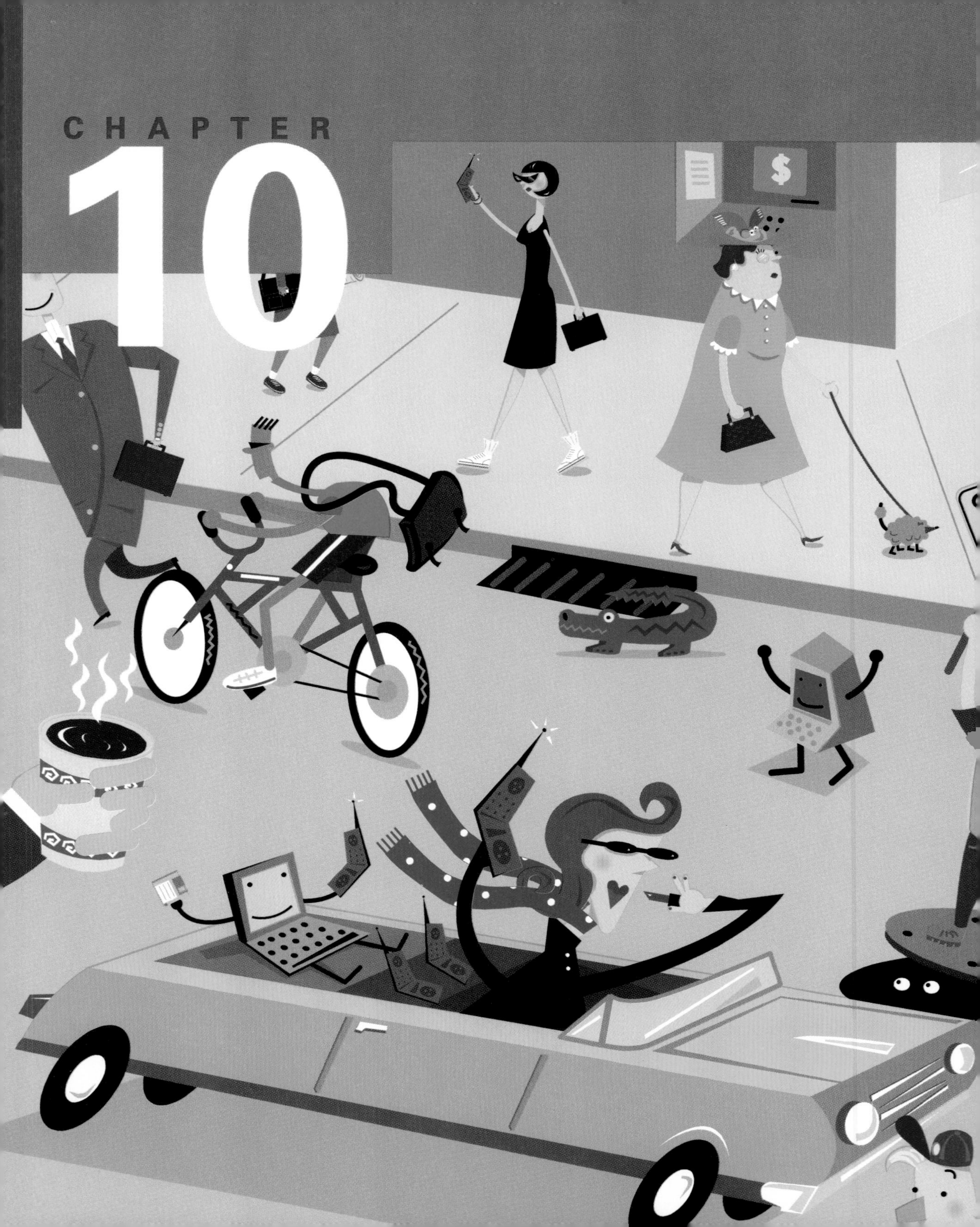

Laying Out Text with Tables

195

Pork vs. Beef
(January - April)

	Pork	Beef
January	23	57
February	48	12
March	23	40
April	36	27

Border line width:	1	pixels
Cell spacing:	2	pixels between cells
Cell padding:	4	pixel space within cells
☑ Table width:	460	Pixels ▼
☑ Table min. height:	30	% of window ▼

☐ Cell Color: [   ] Choose Color

☐ Include caption: ⦿ above ◯ below table

FAST FORWARD

WHAT IS A TABLE? ➤ *pp. 198-200*

- A table is a section of a document divided into rows and columns.
- The intersection of each row and column is called a cell.

INSERT A TABLE INTO YOUR DOCUMENT ➤ *pp. 200-201*

1. Click the Table button.
2. Type a number of rows.
3. Press TAB.
4. Type a number of columns.

FORMAT YOUR TABLE AS YOU INSERT IT ➤ *pp. 201-203*

1. Press TAB to jump to the Border line width box.
2. Type a width for your border and press TAB.
3. Type a number of pixels for spacing between cells and press TAB.
4. Type a number of pixels for spacing within cells.
5. Check Table width.
6. Select Pixels or % of Window.
7. Type a number of pixels or percentage (if not 100).
8. Check Table min. height, if you wish to set one (or skip the next steps if you don't).
9. Select Pixels or % of Window.
10. Type a number of pixels or percentage (if not 100).

FINISH YOUR TABLE ➤ *pp. 203-204*

1. Choose a background color for the table cells, if you want.
2. Choose to add a caption, if you want.
3. Click OK.

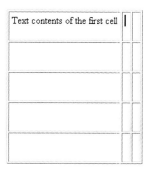

ENTER TEXT IN YOUR TABLE ➤ *pp. 205-207*

1. Position the insertion point in the first cell.
2. Type the contents of that cell.
3. Click in the next cell over.
4. Type the contents of that cell. Repeat as often as necessary.
   - When you are in the last cell of a row, pressing RIGHT ARROW will jump you to the first cell of the next row.
   - If you are in the last cell of the last row, pressing RIGHT ARROW will jump you out of the table.
   - To move back to the previous cell, press LEFT ARROW.

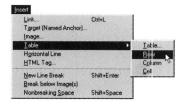

INSERT ROWS, COLUMNS, AND CELLS ➤ *pp. 207-209*

- To insert a row, position the insertion point in the row *above* where you want to insert the new row. Then select Insert I Table I Row.
- To insert a column, position the insertion point in the column *to the left of* where you want to insert the new column. Then select Insert I Table I Column.
- To insert a cell, position the insertion point in the cell *to the left of* where you want to insert the new cell. Then select Insert I Table I Cell.

DELETE ROWS, COLUMNS, AND CELLS ➤ *pp. 209-210*

- To delete a row, position the insertion point in the row and select Edit I Delete Table I Row.
- To delete a column, position the insertion point in the column and select Edit I Delete Table I Column.
- To delete a cell, position the insertion point in the cell and select Edit I Delete Table I Cell.

Graphic designers hate the Web. Why is that? Because it was invented to share academic and scientific information and to standardize documents so that computers can index them easily. This emphasis on content and intention over presentation and cosmetics makes it difficult to design a page layout anywhere near the level of sophistication you might find in your typical print magazine page.

That's why tables were regarded as such a godsend when they were proposed in HTML 3.0 and implemented in Netscape and then later in other browsers. While tables have their own specific purposes, namely the presentation of tabular information (because information is easier to grasp if organized and related spatially), tables can also be used to divide up the page (screen) visually, to simulate margins, side-by-side columns, and more. The Web might never be a complex, page-layout-oriented medium, but tables go a long way toward giving you, as a designer, more control over the positioning of the text and graphics on the page.

If you simply must have more control over the appearance of your documents on the Web, you might consider creating Adobe Acrobat (PDF) documents, as discussed in Chapter 9.

WHAT ARE TABLES?

A table is a section of a document divided into rows and columns. The intersection of each row and column is called a cell. A cell can contain text, hypertext, graphics, and so on, as in the rest of the Web document, or it can be empty. The SYX home page uses a table to arrange various hyperlinks in an asymmetrical pattern. This is achieved by leaving some cells empty (see Figure 10.1).

Tables can have variable-width borders or no borders at all (invisible borders). The relative widths of the columns can be set when the table is created, or they can be changed later. A table can also have a caption (above or below) and headings at the top of each row. Figure 10.2 shows a table with borders, headings, and a caption.

Notice that we are not really dwelling on the tags needed to create tables, since Netscape Editor automates the process for you (and it's a good thing too—tables are about the most complicated things you can

CAUTION

At first it may seem that you can use columns to layout a newspaper-style page, but it won't really work that well. Tables are not the same thing as "snaking columns" and the text in tables cannot reorganize itself to fit entirely in a window. See chapter 11 for how to insert Netscape's new MULTICOL tag.

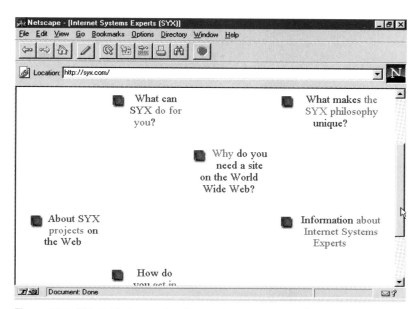

Figure 10.1 This table has no borders and many empty cells

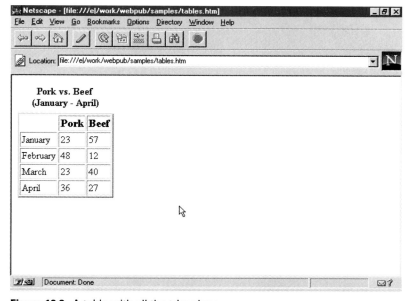

Figure 10.2 A table with all the trimmings

code by hand!). For the record, the basic tags to create a table are the <TABLE> and </TABLE> tags. Within a table, each row starts with <TR> and ends with </TR> and each cell within a row starts with <TD> (for table data) and ends with </TD>. Within and among these tags can be additional tags—for all the special height, width, column- and row-spanning, and other features—which we'll describe in the rest of this chapter.

MAKING TABLES

To insert a table into a Web document click the Table button (or select Insert I Table I Table).

This brings up the New Table Properties dialog box (see Figure 10.3). We'll walk you through the dialog box so you know what you're checking off.

Rows and Columns

First of all, you have to settle on a number of rows and columns. You can change this later, but you should have some idea of how many rows you'll want. For columns, guess big. It's just as easy to trim 'em off the bottom as it is to add new ones there. Sometimes, tables require

habits & strategies

It's a good idea to type some normal text on the page before inserting a table, because it's more difficult to go back later and insert text in front of the table once it's created.

One way to create an indentation or blank space between portions of text is to insert extra columns in your table and keep them blank.

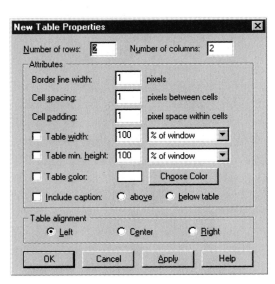

Figure 10.3 Netscape Editor's New Table Properties dialog box makes it easy to fine-tune your table right from the start

one more column and row than you think, especially if you're labeling the contents of the table.

1. Type a number of rows.
2. Press TAB.
3. Type a number of columns.

Borders, Spacing, and Padding

Next, you have to think about the spaces around and between the table's cells. There are three regions you can control: the border around the outside of the table, the spacing between cells, and the padding between the text region inside a cell and its boundary (see Figure 10.4).

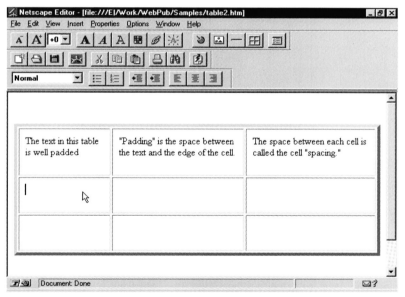

Figure 10.4 This table has a border width of 5, cell spacing of 3, and cell padding of 10

The border defines the exterior boundary of the table visually. Cell spacing can be used to control the layout of the columns. Cell padding keeps the text from running right up against the edge of the cell. For the most part, borders should be kept small. Large borders can look tacky (see Figure 10.5).

*Even if you intend to display
your table with zero borders,
choose a border width of 1
when first creating the table,
or it will be much harder to tell
where each cell of the table is
on your screen. You can
eliminate the border later.
(See "Editing Your Table,"
later in this chapter.)*

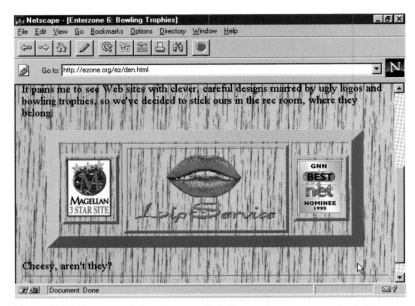

Figure 10.5 *Enterzone's* "trophy room" deliberately uses excessive table border settings to create a tacky look (along with the cheesy wood paneling).

Sometimes, the smoothest effect will be achieved with borders of zero, which will mean no beveled lines between cells or around the outside of the table. This effect can be used to create sophisticated, magazine-style layouts.

1. Press TAB to jump to the Border line width box.
2. Type a width for your border and press TAB.
3. Type a number of pixels for spacing between cells and press TAB.
4. Type a number of pixels for spacing within cells.

Table Width (and Height)

You don't have to set the table's width, but you'll probably want to. If you leave it unspecified, the columns' widths will be determined by the text in the cells. You can set the table width to a specific number of pixels or to a percentage of the width of the screen. The advantage

To make sure your pages will look good on as many screens as possible, design for a lowest-common-denominator, such as the low-resolution PC screen (640 pixels wide and 480 pixels high). The active area of a Web browser is smaller than the entire screen, so don't forget to leave room for the edges and scroll bars of the browsers.

To create margins on a page, you can set the table width to less than 100% and then, later, apply center alignment to the table.

of specifying the width in pixels is that you'll know exactly how wide the table will appear, and you can use this to line up text with graphics or other elements with a fixed width. The disadvantage is that, without knowing any of the other dimensions of your reader's interface (the screen size, the resolution, the size of the fonts), you'll still have, really, no idea how the page is going to look, and you may set a table width that is too wide for some screens.

The advantage of setting a table's width in terms of a percentage is that you'll have some idea of how the table will look relative to any screen width. The disadvantage is that the contents of the table will wrap and fill the cells differently depending on the details of the reader's screen setup, which may destroy any visual effects you were aiming to achieve.

Minimum table height can be set as well, the same way table width is set, but it's much less useful, unless you want to make sure that your table fills the entire screen, for example, or some set percentage of it.

1. Check Table width.
2. Select Pixels or Percent of Window.
3. Type a number of pixels or percentage (if not 100).
4. Check Table min. height, if you wish to set one (or skip the next steps if you don't).
5. Select Pixels or % of Window.
6. Type a number of pixels or percentage (if not 100).

Customized Cell Colors

Although it's conceptually a bit of a non sequitur, you can set a color for the background of the cells in the table (it can be different from the background color on the rest of the page). Figure 10.6 shows a table with cells a different color from that of the page.

1. Click the Choose button.
2. Choose a color from the color dialog box that pops up (or create a custom color, as described in Chapter 8).
3. Click OK.

habits & strategies

Cell colors can be used to create the effect of, say, a blue column down the middle of a white screen, or alternating colored rows.

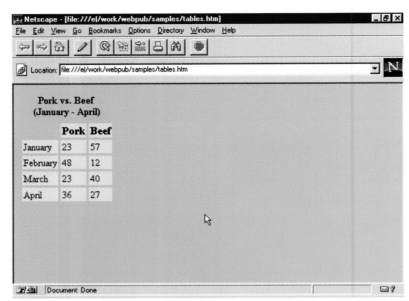

Figure 10.6 You can change the color of the cells in a table to show the shape of the table in a different way

trends

Microsoft has introduced background images for individual cells (see Chapter 8 for more on background images), and before long, Netscape will no doubt support them as well.

Attaching a Caption

A caption is just a bit of text attached to the table that usually describes or introduces it. You can format the text of a caption just as you would normal text.

1. Click Include caption if you want a caption for your table.
2. Click below table if you want the caption to appear below the table instead of above it.

CAUTION

Moving around tables in Netscape Editor is a little trickier than in most word processors. You can easily jump entirely outside of the table if you're not careful. Rely mainly on mouse-clicking and the RIGHT ARROW *and* LEFT ARROW *keys. Also, move slowly and carefully.*

Choosing an Alignment

If the table width is less than the full width of the screen, then you can choose left, Center, or Right alignment. (This is a good way to simulate left and right margins.)

Finishing Your Table

When you've made your way through the dialog box, click OK. Your table will appear (see Figure 10.7).

If it doesn't look exactly the way you pictured it, remember that there's no text in it and you haven't typed a caption yet.

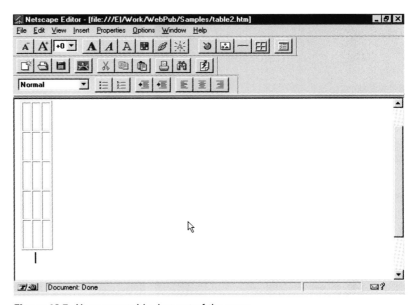

Figure 10.7 Your new table, hot out of the oven

You may find clicking in cells to be the easiest way to get around, especially after you've typed cell contents, when using the arrow keys sometimes means tediously moving through the text of an entire cell before jumping to the next cell.

ENTERING TEXT IN TABLES

To begin entering text in your table, position the insertion point in the first cell and just start typing. The cell will expand to accommodate the text you type. When you are done with the first cell, click in the next cell over, or press the RIGHT ARROW key to jump there.

Cells can contain anything a Web document can contain, not just text. You can insert links, images, and so on. Often the easiest way to place complex material in a table cell is to cut it from a normal Web document and paste it into the cell.

Text contents of the first cell	

Then type the contents of that cell. Repeat as often as necessary. When you are in the last cell of a row, pressing RIGHT ARROW will jump you to the first cell of the next row. If you are in the last cell of the last row, pressing RIGHT ARROW will jump you out of the table. To move back to the previous cell, press LEFT ARROW. To move up one row to the cell immediately above the current cell, press UP ARROW. To move down one row, press DOWN ARROW.

Besides typing the contents of the table, you can also type your caption above or below it. The caption has no special formatting associated with it, so, besides typing it, you should format it as you deem appropriate (make it bold, for example, or center it, and so on).

Most likely, Netscape will continue to develop their table-interface to make it more flexible and fluid. A likely model for how tables might work in the near future is the way major word processing programs, such as Word and WordPerfect do it. They allow you to use all the arrow keys, as well as tabs, and they permit complex cutting and pasting, including multiple-cell selections and movement of table cells, rows, and columns. Web tables don't even currently use the concept of a column, particularly. Tables are divided first into rows and then into cells. If the cells happen to line up into a column, well, great. In the long run, though, the HTML standard and Netscape Editor will probably implement column-formatting features as well.

CAUTION

To view the text of the table "flat out" instead of in table form, select View | Display Tables. Select it again to return to normal table view.

January	23	57
February	48	12
March	23	40
April	36	27

You can cut, copy, and paste text to and from table cells, but a selection cannot cross a cell border. Therefore, you can't, for example, copy the contents of two cells from one place to another at the same time. You have to move the content piecemeal. You can only cut, copy, and paste cell contents, not the actual cell, row, or table structure.

EDITING YOUR TABLE

Once you've entered the text in your table, you'll inevitably want to make changes. The way you edit text in a table is not terribly different from how you do it in a normal Web document. You can make selections within cells and delete them, or cut, copy, or paste them. If you make a selection that crosses a cell boundary and then try to delete or cut the selection, Netscape Editor warns you that this is not permitted:

You may also want to change the very structure of your table. As we mentioned before, when you first create your table, you're not locking yourself into the exact dimensions you initially pick. As you edit and sometimes rethink table content, you might eventually want to change the number of rows or columns, or even cells in a specific row. Netscape editor makes it pretty easy to insert or delete any table element.

Inserting

To insert a row, position the insertion point in the row *above* where you want to insert the new row. Then select Insert | Table | Row. Netscape Editor inserts a new blank row below the row containing the insertion point. The new row has the same number of cells with the same formatting as the row above. Now type the text for the new row.

You can't insert a new row at the top of a table, directly. To work around this limitation, put the insertion point in the top row and insert two rows (one after another). Type the contents for your intended top row in the first of the two new rows. Then copy, cell by cell, the contents of the old first row into the second new row. Finally, delete the old top row, as explained in the next section.

To insert a column, position the insertion point in the column *to the left of* where you want to insert the new column. Then select Insert I Table I Column. Netscape Editor inserts a new blank column to the right of the column containing the insertion point. The new column has the same number of cells with the same formatting as the column to the left. Now type the text for the new column.

As with rows, you can't directly insert a new column at the left side of a table. Put the insertion point in the leftmost column and insert two columns (one after another). Type the contents for your intended left column in the first of the two new columns. Then copy, cell by cell, the contents of the old first column into the second new column. Finally, delete the old leftmost column, as explained in the next section.

	Pork	Beef
January	23	57
February	48	12
March	23	40
April	36	27

Because each row is allowed to contain a different number of cells, you can also insert a cell into any row. This will generally necessitate the creation of a new column containing only a single cell. To insert a cell, position the insertion point in the cell *to the left of* where you want to insert the new cell. Then select Insert I Table I Cell. Netscape Editor inserts a new blank cell to the right of the cell containing the insertion point and pushes each cell to the right of the new cell over one cell to the right.

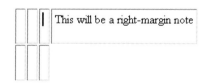

This will be a right-margin note

habits & strategies

"Orphan" cells, like the one shown here, can be used to create special layout elements, such as notes in a margin.

Now type the text for the new cell.

It's also possible to insert an entire table into a cell of another table. This enables you to get really creative with your layout, when you can align text in columns and rows *within* a bigger arrangement of cells.

To insert a table into an existing table, put the insertion point in the cell where you want the new table to appear and click the Insert Table button or select Insert I Table I Table. This brings up the New Table Properties dialog box shown in Figure 10.3. Follow the instructions in Making Tables, earlier in this chapter, to complete the inserted table. Figure 10.8 shows a Web page that uses a table within a table.

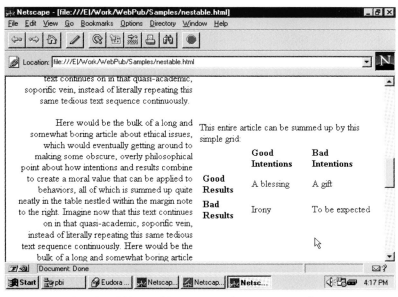

Figure 10.8   A table within a table can sometimes cure your layout headaches

Deleting

To delete a row, position the insertion point in the row and select Edit I Delete Table I Row. Netscape Editor deletes the row. If you change your mind, select Edit I Undo.

To delete a column, position the insertion point in the column and select Edit I Delete Table I Column. Netscape Editor deletes the column.

To delete a cell, position the insertion point in the cell and select Edit I Delete Table I Cell. Netscape Editor deletes the cell and moves any cells to its right one position to the left.

CAUTION

Undo does not always work perfectly with tables, sometimes mangling the format slightly. So be careful when you are deleting anything in a table.

When deleting a table within a table, be very careful to place the insertion point in the inner table. Otherwise, you will delete both the inner table and the main table.

(month)	Pork	Beef
January	23	57
February	48	12
23	40	
April	36	27

To delete an entire table, or a table within a table, put the insertion point in the table you want to delete and then select Edit I Delete Table I Table. The table is gone.

Moving Rows and Cells

There's no way to cut and paste entire rows or columns, or multiple cells at one time. The only way to achieve the goal of moving a portion of a table is to insert a new row, column, or cells, as described in an earlier section, cut and paste the contents of each cell, one at a time, and then delete the vacated row, column, or cell. And then repeat this as often as necessary.

FORMATTING YOUR TABLE

As with editing, there are two aspects to formatting a table—formatting the text (in the traditional sense), and formatting the elements of the table itself (the rows, columns, and cells). If all you want is to make some of the text in a table bold, for instance, you can just select the text and click the Bold button, as you would normally. (For the purposes of applying formatting, you *can* select the contents of more than one cell at a time.)

To format the table itself, you just drop by the Table Properties dialog box. First, place the insertion point in the specific cell, row, or table you want to affect. Then, either select Properties I Table or right-click on the table (on the Mac, click and hold down the mouse button) and choose Table Properties from the menu that pops up.

The Table Properties dialog divides its options up into three

habits & strategies

If you want to apply any formatting consistently to an entire table, such as raising the size of the text by one unit, you can first choose Edit | Select Table.

tabs: Table, Row, and Cell. The Table tab simply restates the original formatting options you saw when you created the table, so we'll leave that till last.

Formatting a Row

To control alignment or color in a single row, click the Row tab of the Table Properties dialog box (see Figure 10.9).

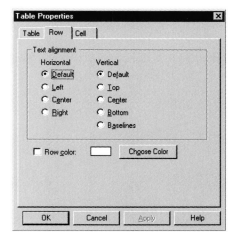

Figure 10.9 There are two things you can control at the row level: alignment and color

Alignment

There are two kinds of alignment in a row, horizontal and vertical. The default horizontal alignment is left. The default vertical alignment is center. If you have a specific position for your text, you should specify it and not rely on defaults, which might produce different results in different browsers. Most of the time, for example, you'll probably want Top vertical alignment instead of the default.

Color

To specify a different background color for an entire row, click the Choose Color button. The Color dialog box will appear. Choose a color—or create a custom color, as described in Chapter 7. Then click OK.

Formatting a Single Cell

To control alignment or color in a single cell, click the Cell tab of the Table Properties dialog box (see Figure 10.10).

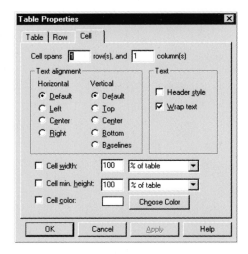

Figure 10.10 There are many things you can control at the cell level, but probably the most important is Cell Width, since you can use it to control the layout of the page

Spanning Cells

One neat trick you can do with tables is create cells that span one or more columns *or* rows (or both). In an orientation similar to the other table formatting commands, cells made to span multiple columns or rows "expand" to the right or down, respectively. Here's a table with a header cell spanning three columns:

Pork vs. Beef (January - April)		
(month)	**Pork**	**Beef**
January	23	57
February	48	12
March	23	40
April	36	27

Cells can span rows as well.

Alignment

Cells have all the same alignment options as rows. This means that you can set general alignment for a row and then change the specific alignment for a particular cell (or cells).

Headers and Wrapping

There are two commands lumped together in the poorly named Text area of the dialog box: Header Style and Wrap Text. By default, Header Style is turned off (unless the row you're in was created as a header) and Wrap Text is turned on.

Checking Header Style just turns the current cell or row into a header, which is mainly a conceptual distinction (although it may center the header text, in some browsers).

Unchecking Wrap Text will cause the text in affected cells to stay on a single line, even if that means being cut off by the limited size of a cell.

Width

You may notice, as you enter text into tables, that the columns adjust themselves for some sort of "best fit" based on the current text as entered. This is fine for an ad hoc table, but not so good if you're trying to lay out the page with some regular column widths or proportions. That's why the width option is the most important one in this dialog box (at least if you're using tables to create a page layout, that is).

To fix the width of selected cells, first check Cell width, then either choose Pixels or keep the % of table option in the drop-down list box. Finally, enter a number of pixels or a percentage of the table width (if not 100).

Repeat this process on as many cells as necessary to fix the proportions of the table. Figure 10.11 shows a Web page that uses a table with fixed columns to create a pleasing layout.

habits & strategies

To give an entire table consistent proportions, you can either select a column at a time and choose the width settings, or you can start with a one-row table, set widths for all the cells, and then create the rest of the rows by inserting them after the first "template" row.

CAUTION

Don't get too clever and fancy in your use of multiple colors in tables, or you'll create a busy, distracting effect.

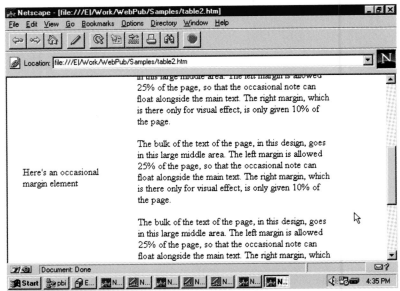

Figure 10.11 The page is divided into three columns, a medium-sized left column, a large middle column for the basic text of the page, and a small right-margin column

Minimum Height

If you need a selected cell, row, or entire tableful of cells to have a specific height, either in terms of absolute number of pixels or as a percentage of the table's height, you can check Cell min. height. Then choose Pixels or % of Table, and then enter a number (if not 100).

Color

As with all the other table dialog boxes, the Cell tab of the Table Properties dialog box allows you to select a background cell color for the selected cells. Click the Choose Color button, choose a color from the Color dialog box that pops up, and then click OK.

Rethinking Overall Table Format

To reconsider the overall formatting of the table (such as the choices you made when you first created the table), click the Table tab on the Table Properties dialog box. The Table tab recaps all the options available when you first created the table, except for the numbers of rows and columns.

CONVERTING BETWEEN TEXT AND TABLES

Unlike many word processing programs, Netscape Editor can't automatically convert between a table format and a regular text format. Instead, if you have text in some plain style (or organized as preformatted—what Netscape calls Formatted—text), you have to create the table first, in a blank space, and then cut and paste the text elements into the table by hand. Likewise, to convert table text back into some straightforward layout, you have to "rescue" all the text from the table, once cell at a time, and then delete the table when you're done.

WHAT'S NEXT?

What makes the Web so much more exciting than almost every other aspect of the Internet? The pictures, of course. And, to a lesser extent, the ability to download almost any type of file by just selecting a link. In the next two chapters, we'll show you the ins and out of placing graphics on your pages, and then how to incorporate any other type of medium into a Web document.

Tailoring Your Site for Specific Browsers

FAST FORWARD

NETSCAPE EDITOR TAGS NOT RECOGNIZED BY ALL BROWSERS ➤ *pp. 220-221*

- Font size and color tags
- Centering and right-alignment tags
- Horizontal rule features

HTML Tag

Enter tag name and any attributes or parameters for one tag only.

```
<center><p>
<br><hr size=6 width="60%" >
<br><font SIZE=+2>In this design, pull quotes a
<br>off with centered, less-than-full-
<br>width, large-sized horizontal rules.</font>
<br>
<br><hr size=5 width="60%" >
<hr size=3 width="60%" ></p></center>
```

INSERT A SINGLE HTML TAG ➤ *pp. 221-222*

1. Select Insert I HTML Tag.
2. Type the tag you want to insert (or copy and paste HTML from some other source).
3. Click OK.

INSERT A LOT OF HTML AT ONCE ➤ *pp. 222-224*

1. Select View I Edit Document Source.
2. Set up a text editor for Netscape Editor, if prompted.
3. Type (or copy and paste) whatever HTML you want to insert directly into your document.
4. Save your work.
5. Close the editor.
6. When you switch back to Netscape Editor, it will realize that the underlying HTML source file has changed and offer to reload it.
7. Click Yes.

It is commonly thought that one should design for the widest possible audience on the Web. Of course this is true. You should never, within reason, limit your audience. On the other hand, for the near future it seems clear that Netscape Navigator (and any other browser that works about the same way) is going to be the standard Web browser for a majority of users on the Internet.

Many Web designers have given in to the temptation to design specifically for Netscape, often with that maddening free ad—"this Web Site best viewed with Netscape Navigator version 5.6 alpha 0.2b. Click 'here' to download it now !!!" So, you must strike a balance somewhere in between.

It *is* possible to selectively enhance a site with elements catering to a specific browser and not alienate the rest of your audience. The way to do this is to use only those elements that don't "break" other browsers (meaning ones that don't ruin the rest of the HTML and screw up the layout of the page).

Naturally, Netscape Editor favors Netscape extensions over those introduced by other sources. But interestingly, the Editor module does not even have commands for all of the HTML tags that the Netscape Navigator browser module recognizes. For this reason, we'll show you how to add in any specific HTML tag you want, even if Netscape Editor doesn't know it from <ADAM>. Finally, we'll fill you in on some of the Netscape and Microsoft extensions to HTML and HTML 3.2 (the next version of HTML after 2.0, which was the last one that all browsers agreed on), and tell you which of those features Navigator can read as well.

habits & strategies

To make sure your innovations don't break other browsers, try viewing your Web documents in several different browsers.

NETSCAPE HTML AND OTHER BROWSER SUPPORT

The formatting commands explained in Chapter 5 dealt mainly with Netscape extensions to HTML. Not all of these features are supported by every type of browser. In this section we'll caution you about tags that are not fully supported.

habits & strategies

You can also change font size with the HTML 3.2 commands <BIG> and <SMALL>, which Netscape recognizes, but which are not as widely accepted as the <FONT SIZE=...> tag.

bookmark

*Netscape offers complete listings of the various flavors of HTML at the HTML Language Specification (**http://developer.netscape.com/platform/ html_compilation/index.html**). For an excellent reference comparing the tags in HTML 2.0, Netscape-extended HTML, Internet Explorer-extended HTML, and HTML 3.x, see the Bare Bones Guide to HTML (**http://werbach.com/barebones/barebone_table.html**). Print it out! For more on which browsers support which HTML tags, see the BrowserCaps site (**http://objarts.com/bc/**).*

Font Formatting

Not every Web browser recognizes the FONT SIZE commands. In fact some, such as Lynx, have no way of changing text size. This generally shouldn't cause you any design problems as long as the functionality of your design doesn't hinge on text size. (You may, for example, end up with lines that look too long or too short in other browsers.)

Browsers that don't recognize FONT SIZE= also don't recognize the BASEFONT SIZE= tag. Also, many browsers don't recognize the FONT COLOR= commands.

CAUTION

Many other types of browsers (including any version of Netscape Navigator prior to 2.0) will neither recognize nor display spot text color, so don't base anything intrinsically vital in your design on this feature. Use it as a "treat" for the people who can appreciate it.

Left alignment is the default for most elements in every browser, so there's usually no harm if the ALIGN=LEFT tag is omitted.

Alignment Options

In order to give you a full range of alignment options, Netscape Editor mixes the Netscape HTML extension <CENTER> tag with the ALIGN=LEFT, RIGHT, or CENTER features that can be attached to most tags in HTML 3.2. Many Web browsers do not recognize ALIGN=RIGHT yet, so if you design using this feature, check your page in several browsers.

Horizontal Rules

The extra controls for horizontal rules that Netscape Editor offers are not standard HTML 2.0 features. Fortunately, any browser that doesn't recognize the SIZE, WIDTH, or NOSHADE attributes will still insert a normal horizontal rule any time it sees <HR, followed by anything and ending with >. If your design relies on clever use of horizontal rule tweaking, then it may lose a lot in translation on non-Netscape browsers.

Netscape Editor does not have commands for *every* type of formatting that Navigator can display correctly. For example, the 3.0 version of Netscape Editor does not include a frame editor, even though Netscape Navigator can certainly display frames. If you want to insert a Netscape-specific tag that Netscape Editor does not offer (such as table formatting), you can still enter the exact tags directly. This method is also useful for inserting Internet Explorer and HTML 3.2 tags as well.

INSERTING HTML TAGS BY HAND

If you want to include any HTML elements that are not provided by Netscape Editor, you can do so, but you'll have to type in the tags yourself. For individual HTML tags, just select Insert I HTML Tag. This brings up the HTML Tag dialog box.

221

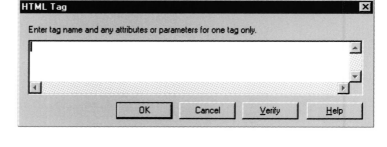

You can only enter one tag at a time.

Type the tag you want to insert (or copy and paste HTML from some other source) and then click OK. Netscape Editor can't properly interpret the tag you insert, but it will insert this symbol to remind you that there's some "extra" HTML in your document:

If you want to insert a great deal of HTML coding (and regular text) at the same time, select View I Edit Document Source. If you've never selected this command before, Netscape will alert you that you haven't selected an external HTML editor yet. Click Yes. The Editor Preferences dialog box will appear with the General tab selected (see Figure 11.1).

In the HTML source box in the External editors area, either type the file name (preceded by a path, if necessary) of your favorite text or raw-HTML editor, or click the Browse button, hunt around for it, and click OK. Then click OK to close the Editor Preferences dialog box.

Then type (or copy and paste) whatever HTML you want to insert directly into your document (see Figure 11.2).

When you're done, save your work and close the editor. When you switch back to Netscape Editor, it will realize that the underlying HTML source file has changed and offer to reload it. Click Yes.

If Netscape recognizes the tags you entered, it will try to interpret and display them. If it does not recognize them, then it will simply insert starting and ending HTML marker symbols into your document.

⟨If Netscape Editor doesn't recognize the codes you inserted manually, it will represent them with symbols.⟨/⟩

habits & strategies

On the PC, WordPad (usually C:\Program Files\Accessories\Wordpad.exe) is a good choice for an editor. On the Mac, SimpleText will do.

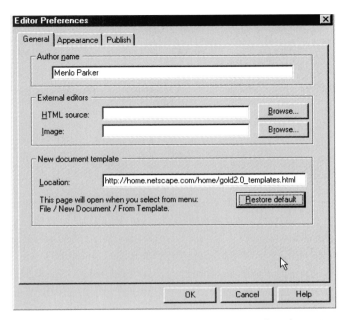

Figure 11.1 Type, insert, or browse for the name of your favorite text or HTML editor

Netscape Editor changes some tags automatically, which you might not want it to do. For example, if you insert <CITE> and </CITE>, it will change them to <I> and </I>, which might look the same in some browsers, but which means something different. It also seems to enter an extra <P> and </P> here and there in your document.

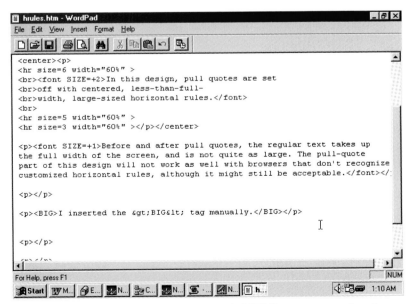

Figure 11.2 You can insert as much extended HTML as you want directly into your document this way

If you double-click on one of these symbols, it will open up the HTML Tag dialog box, allowing you to edit the particular tag.

Even if you insert <FONT FACE=""> commands into your documents manually, they will be eliminated by Netscape Editor the next time you edit your document. So, you have to do it last, at least until a newer release of Netscape Gold eliminates this "feature."

If you position the mouse pointer over one of these symbols, the status bar will show the underlying, unorthodox tag.

If Netscape Editor doesn't recognize the codes you inserted manually, it will represent them with symbols.

`</BANNER>`

Font Color Names and Typefaces

Microsoft's Internet Explorer has not introduced as many new HTML tags as Netscape Navigator has, but there are a few you might want to use. One, which has already been picked up by Netscape Editor, is a set of 16 colors that can be described by name instead of by numerical methods (from which you've been shielded by the Color picker dialog box). These color names are Aqua, Black, Blue, Fuschia, Gray, Green, Lime, Maroon, Navy, Olive, Purple, Red, Silver, Teal, White, and Yellow.

bookmark

*The complete list of Internet Explorer extensions to HTML can be found by poking around at **http://www.microsoft.com/ie/**. (Warning: They change their addresses a lot at that site.)*

Another feature just added to Netscape Navigator is the ability to specify a series of alternative typefaces (also commonly referred to as fonts), in order of preference, with the <FONT FACE="*first choice, second choice, third choice, and so on*"> tag.

Netscape Editor is not capable of inserting the FONT FACE specification, so if you're interested in trying to use it, you'll have to edit your documents as text files, using a text editor.

To specify a font for a selection of text, precede it with the tag <FONT FACE="*font name [, optional list of font names, ...]*"> and follow it with </FONT>. So, for example, you could suggest three recommended fonts for a selection as follows:

```
<FONT FACE="Palatino, Garamond, Times New Roman">Is this Palatino?</FONT>
```

habits & strategies

For text already marked with the FONT tag (such as colored or resized text), you can simply add the FACE="" tag to the existing tag, as in <FONT SIZE="+1" COLOR="FF0000" FACE="Arial">

Body Codes

Internet Explorer introduced a couple of new attributes associated with the body of a Web document. The most interesting one makes it possible to use a background image that stays still when you scroll through the document. To get this effect, you have to insert the following attribute into the <BODY> tag:

```
BGPROPERTIES=fixed
```

You can also, optionally, specify an indentation from the left or top margins with either of the LEFTMARGIN= or TOPMARGIN= commands, with the indentation space specified in pixels.

New, One-Off Netscape Codes

Navigator 3.0 introduces some new Netscape-specific codes that are not yet available from Netscape Editor. Table 11.1 shows a quick rundown. None of these codes are yet supported by any other browsers.

Another body attribute introduced by Internet Explorer is the BGSOUND (background sound) tag, which specifies a sound file to play when a reader visits the document. See Chapter 9 for more on incorporating various media into a Web site.

Code	What it Does
<MULTICOL COLS=*n* GUTTER=*x* WIDTH=*y*>...</MULTICOL>	Sets up multiple snaking columns on the screen (only the COLS attribute is required).
<SPACER TYPE=HORIZONAL, VERTICAL, *or* BLOCK SIZE=*x or* HEIGHT=*m* WIDTH=*n* ALIGN=LEFT, CENTER, RIGHT, *and others*>	Inserts horizontal or vertical blank space, with attributes similar to those of the IMG tag. The default type is horizontal.

Table 11.1 Netscape-specific codes in Navigator 3.0

HTML 3.2 and Beyond

There have now been many versions of HTML. The last version that most browsers agreed on was HTML 2.0. (HTML 1.0 was around before almost anyone had ever heard of the Web.) Then there was an ad hoc extended version of HTML 2.0 called HTML+. When Netscape came along, it started introducing new HTML features without running them by the committees that had been set up in the Internet community to keep the development of HTML standardized. While this initially rubbed some people the wrong way, almost all of the Netscape extensions were eventually adopted.

Meanwhile, a parallel set of extensions to HTML 2.0 were codified under the name HTML 3.0. HTML 3.0 was never officially adopted, although some of it trickled into de facto use in browsers. (For example, Navigator versions 2.0 and higher have recognized the 3.0 text size tags <BIG> and <SMALL>.) Then Microsoft Internet Explorer came along, with innovations of its own and, all the while, Netscape continued to throw new elements into the mix all the time.

In May of 1996, the W3 Consortium released a new HTML standard, called HTML 3.2 (no one seems to know what happened to 3.1!). It incorporates all of HTML 2.0, Netscape, and Microsoft extensions, and the least controversial 3.0 codes, but it represents nothing more than a codification of the current state of HTML. Undoubtedly, the standard will keep evolving.

trends

With HTML 3.2 standardizing extensions to 2.0, we can expect both the major browsers (Navigator and Internet Explorer), along with other upstarts, to continue "freelancing"—pioneering new elements in the hopes of attracting an audience.

If you want to enter HTML 3.2 codes that Netscape Editor doesn't recognize, then you'll have to enter them, as with any other HTML extensions, directly into the HTML source of your Web document.

Standardized Alignment

Different HTML extensions have offered different methods for aligning portions of documents. In HTML 3.2, there's a standard ALIGN= [LEFT, RIGHT, *or* CENTER] tag that can be included in just about any tag (but for now it's mainly limited to <P>, <IMG>, and <DIV>, to be discussed next). In addition to the ALIGN= tag, there's a new tag that can be used to delineate any section of a document and then set its alignment (or other attributes). The new tag is called DIV (for division), and takes this simple form:

```
<DIV ALIGN=RIGHT>
This section of the document is right-aligned
</DIV>
```

Text Elements

A few new text-formatting elements have been introduced or standardized in HTML 3.2. These include: <BIG> and <SMALL>, each of which bump the surrounded text up or down one size; <SUB> (subscript) and <SUP> (superscript); <STRIKE> (also, just <S>), to create strike-through text (to denote edits, as in some legal documents); and <U>, for underlining.

WHAT'S NEXT?

The next chapter will give you a foothold into creating (or hiring out to create) most of the bells and whistles that distinguish today's sophisticated sites from run-of-the-mill home pages. This includes making image maps, assembling frames, putting together forms, and finding scripts to make everything work together. Chapter 13 will tell you what you need to know about Web servers.

CHAPTER

12

Web Wizardry: Navigation Aids and Dynamic Scripts

INCLUDES

- Image Maps

- Basic Frames

- Forms

- CGI Scripts

- JavaScript Tricks

229

FAST FORWARD

THREE WAYS TO CREATE IMAGE MAPS ➤ *pp. 233-238*

- For traditional, server-side maps, create a map reference file and post it to your Web server (see Chapter 13 for more on servers).
- For a new wave, client-side image map, use the <MAP> and </MAP> tags to designate hot regions on the map (within the HTML coding of the document containing the map), and add a USEMAP="*name*" command to the <IMG> tag for the map graphic.
- For a "fake" image map, cut your image up into a series of graphics and insert them each as borderless hyperlinks, one right next to the other.

PUT FRAMES ON YOUR PAGES ➤ *pp. 239-242*

1. Come up with a simple frame design (such as a small navigation frame and a large contents frame).
2. Find a good page on the Net with an example you'd like to follow.
3. Use the View | Document Source and View | Frame Source tags to see how your model works.
4. Copy or adapt the tags to your own purposes.

Your Name: yername here

Submit Reset

BUILD A FORM ➤ *pp. 242-246*

1. Start with <FORM METHOD=GET *or* PUT ACTION="*URL of script for form*">.
2. Put buttons in your form with <INPUT TYPE="submit" VALUE="*optional text, instead of 'Submit'*"> and <INPUT TYPE="reset" VALUE="*optional text, instead of 'Reset'*">.
3. To make the form itself, use the following tags:
   * <TEXTAREA NAME="*name*" ROWS=*x* COLS=*y*>*optional suggested default text*</TEXTAREA>
   * <INPUT NAME="*name*" TYPE="text, password, checkbox, radio, int, hidden, submit, reset" VALUE="*default value, if any*" SIZE="*optional size*" MAXLENGTH="*optional maximum length*">
   * <SELECT NAME="*name*" SIZE="*optional number of items to be shown at a time*"> ... </SELECT>
4. End with </FORM>.
5. Find and install a script to make the form work (that's the catch), or find someone to do it for you.

If you've made it this far through the book, then you're already something of an expert on Web publishing. You know how to build pages, format them, put links in them, put art on them, and even incorporate other media into them. This chapter will cover some of the more advanced bells and whistles that adorn the heppest pages. If you're satisfied with what you already know how to do, and you're anxious to get your pages out there on the Net for public consumption, then skip ahead to Chapter 13 to learn how to publish your site and promote it responsibly on the Internet.

If you're looking for that extra bit of gloss to set your pages apart from the rest, or at least from your competitors, then stick around. This chapter covers two major areas of sophisticated Web site design. The first is navigation. You already know how to insert hyperlinks into pages; both text and image links. Here we'll show you how to make an image map (a graphic that takes the audience to different destinations depending on where it's clicked), and how to set up a simple page with frames. Frames are tricky and have all sorts of subtleties; there's no way we can give you a full tutorial on all of their ins and outs (especially since you have to do all the coding by hand). But we'll explain the principles involved, show you the HTML tags that make frames work, and point you to some useful examples on the Web.

In the second half of the chapter, we'll give you some idea of how to make your pages *dynamic*. Most Web documents are *static*. They are pages not terribly unlike printed pages, except for the embedded links. Dynamic pages are pages that do something in response to the reader's actions (something beyond just jumping you to a different page). The most common sort of dynamic pages are forms. Depending on how the reader fills out a form, different results are generated. To account for these different possibilities, you need to set up *scripts*.

habits & strategies

Just like most people learned HTML in the early days—by viewing source documents to see what tags made them tick— so too do many Web developers cadge their ideas for frames and scripts by looking at other sites and how their codes are set up.

Scripts are simple little programs that run either on the client's machine or at the server end and make actions occur in response to circumstances. It would take an entire book, longer than this one, to teach you all about scripting. The most we can do is explain the concept and show you some examples. For simple goals, you can steal—that is, borrow—working examples from the Web and reuse them. For more elaborate goals, you'll need to nab yourself a real programmer to do the scripting and, more importantly, install the scripts and *debug* them so they really work.

SOPHISTICATED NAVIGATION TRICKS

Besides the basic technique for helping readers navigate— supplying each page with consistently organized hyperlinks—there are a few newer kinds of guides that have caught on. The first is the image map, which can send a reader, depending on where they click the map, to different locations. The second is frames. Frames ostensibly just divide up Web documents into independent sections (sort of like a TV dinner!), but their real purpose is to designate some sections of the screen for certain purposes (for navigation or other control panels, banners and headers, and so on), while reserving some for other purposes (such as displaying the primary content of the site).

Image Maps and Three Ways to Make Them

Most image maps are graphical versions of what you might call a key-word index. They often show some form of illustration with format-ted text on top. Depending on what word or button you click, you will be sent to a different destination. That's the typical sort of image map, but it's not the only type. Image maps can also be used creatively to supply a graphical depiction of a place with a number of different links. Figure 12.1 shows the image map from a Web article called "An Unguided Tour of Pompeii." Clicking on different areas of the map sends the readers to different photographic essays showing various parts of the Pompeii archeological dig site.

habits & strategies

Bear in mind that people with non-graphical browsers (or those browsing with image-loading turned off) will not be able to use your image map! (Unless you create a fake one, as explained at the end of this section.) Be sure to give them some kind of text alternative. We'll show you how for each type of map.

Naturally, image maps can also be heavily pictorial, incorporating any of the GIF or JPEG effects possible for normal images. See Chapter 8 for more on graphics.

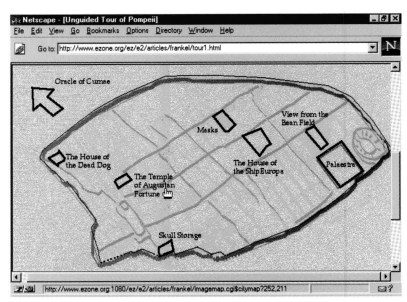

Figure 12.1 This simplified map of Pompeii functions as a graphical doorway to the various entries about the archeological site (See the *x* and *y* coordinates in the status bar?)

Most of the time, you'll use maps to lead readers to the major categories of pages at your site. The first step then, in the creation of any image map, is the production of the artwork. If you want something as basic as plain formatted text or a simple graphic, you can assemble the image yourself. If you want something more sophisticated, you may need to hire a graphic artist.

Here's a simple image map graphic using the same font as the logo of the pages it will go on and a simple black-on-white color scheme with no background art:

What makes a map work is that different regions of the image are assigned to different URLs. (You usually also assign a default address to go to, in case the reader clicks somewhere on the image but outside any of the "hot" regions.)

**h a b i t s &
s t r a t e g i e s**

*Be sure to make the border for
the image map graphic equal to
zero unless you want a blue (or
other-colored) line surrounding
your image map.*

*You can remove the ISMAP attribute
from within Netscape Editor by clicking
the Remove Image Map button on the
Image tab of the Properties dialog box.*

Traditional Server-Side Maps

The original type of image map is a graphic that tells the browser it's a map. When clicked, the browser sends to the Web site's server the exact coordinates of the image to which the mouse was pointing (x and y, so many pixels over from the left edge, so many pixels down from the top edge). The server then consults a map file to see what document or other object to send back to the browser.

In the document itself, you first insert the image map as you would any other graphic (see Chapter 8). But then you have to edit the image tag to tell browsers that it's an image map. To do this, select View | Edit Document Source.

In the window that appears, find the image tag for the image you just inserted. It will look something like this:

```
<center><p>
<hr size=4>
<img src="navmap.GIF" height=50 width=400>
```

Position the insertion point just inside the closing > (greater-than sign) and type the tag **ISMAP** there.

```
<center><p>
<hr size=4>
<img src="navmap.GIF" height=50 width=400 BORDER=0 ISMAP>
```

Then save the change and close the text-editing window. Netscape Editor will ask you if it should reload the edited file. Click Yes.

Next, you have to make the image a link as well—a link to the image map reference file. (You can add the link and then create the file or do it in the other order.) You make the link just as you would any graphical link (as explained in Chapter 8), by clicking the Link tab in the Properties dialog box and entering the URL for the file.

That was the easy part. To make this sort of image map work, you'll need access to your server to put the reference file there. See Chapter 13 for more about servers and working with service providers. Really, though, the file that the server looks up when the image map is clicked is just a simple list of shapes (rectangles, circles, and polygons), URLs, and coordinates. It's possible to create such a file by hand, by

habits & strategies

To minimize the distraction for readers using graphical browsers, you can make the text links very small. Plain text browsers such as Lynx will display the text at full size anyway.

If you're not sure how to insert tags into a Web document, see Chapter 11.

figuring out the dimensions of the various regions of your map and typing up the file. A line in such a file would look something like this:

```
rect http://syx.com/ 0,0 88,50
```

Then again, you may find it easier to use one of the many shareware tools available online for creating image maps. Most of them work by displaying your graphic and inviting you to draw shapes on it (as you would in a simple paintbrush-type graphics program). When you're done, the program you use will output the appropriate file.

bookmark

*Two good image-map tools for Windows are MapEdit (**http://www.boutell.com/mapedit/**) and Map THIS (**http://galadriel.ecaetc.ohio-state.edu/tc/mt**). For the Macintosh, try WebMap (**http://www.city.net/cnx/software/webmap.html**).*

OK, so now where do you put this reference file? That depends on how your server is set up and the administrator or Webmaster of your site should be able to tell you.

Then you have to address non-graphical browsers. For an image map, a set of plain text links just below the map, such as the following, is a decent alternative:

[Home | Info | Services | Sites | Mail]

The key words themselves can be links to the appropriate destinations.

If all of this sounds a little too tricky, consider one of the easier types of image maps to create, described in the remainder of this section.

New Client-Side Maps

It's silly, really, to go to the server to figure out the meaning of an image map click, when the browser could do the job just as well and faster. Spyglass, one of the commercial developers of Mosaic, proposed a new

CAUTION

The ALT attribute is not correctly implemented in some browsers.

type of image map that lets the browser sort things out. These maps are called client-side image maps, because the "thinking" is done on the client, or browser, side of the transaction, instead of on the server end. Netscape and Microsoft quickly incorporated client-side image map recognition into their subsequent releases of Navigator and Internet Explorer, so this type of map is fairly safe to use. It also provides for alternative text for each region of the map.

A client-side image map has two parts, the description of the map areas (using the new <MAP> tag) and the image (using a new addition to the <IMG ... > tag, called USEMAP). A map description also has to have a NAME description that starts with <MAP NAME="*mapname*"> and ends with </MAP>. The NAME attribute works just like the named target anchors in Chapter 7.

Between the MAP tags, you include an <AREA ...> tag for each region of the map. The AREA tag includes the following additional tags:

- SHAPE="RECT", "CIRCLE", *or* "POLYGON"
- COORDS="*x1,y1,x2,y2*"
- HREF="*destination URL*"
- ALT="*alternative text*"

So, for example, the MAP description for an image map might look like this:

```
<MAP NAME="navmap">
<AREA SHAPE="RECT" COORDS="0, 0, 88, 50" HREF="index.html" ALT="[ Home ">
<AREA SHAPE="RECT" COORDS="88, 0, 171, 50" HREF="info.html" ALT="| Info ">
<AREA SHAPE="RECT" COORDS="171, 0, 234, 50" HREF="svcs.html" ALT="| Services |">
<AREA SHAPE="RECT" COORDS="234, 0, 317, 50" HREF="sites.html" ALT=" Sites |">
<AREA SHAPE="RECT" COORDS="317, 0, 400, 50" HREF="mailbag.html" ALT=" Mail ]">
</MAP>
```

If there is a "no man's land" on your map that sends readers to some default page, just add one additional AREA tag at the end of the list and give it coordinates that include the entire image. (The areas defined earlier take precedence.)

Don't forget to type a # before the map's name.

The MAP description can go anywhere in the document. But to make it actually work, you have to add the USEMAP="#*mapname*" tag to the IMG tag for the image map, like so:

```
<IMG SRC="navmap.gif" USEMAP="#navmap">
```

How to Fake an Image Map

You can also make a quick and dirty image map just by slicing up a graphic into pieces and then inserting them side by side into your document. Make sure each image-piece has no border—and no horizontal spacing, for that matter—and make each piece a link to the destination it corresponds to. Add alternative text as you would to any image.

Figure 12.2 shows two pieces of a "fake" image map inserted into a Web document.

This method, naturally, requires no special cooperation from the server, so it's sort of the ultimate client-side image map.

CAUTION

This method really only works for straightforward image maps in which each region is a contiguous slice of an image. It would be quite difficult to "fake" the image map of Pompeii shown earlier, for example. Also, it increases significantly the aggregate file size of the image, since each "slice" bears the overhead of an entire image.

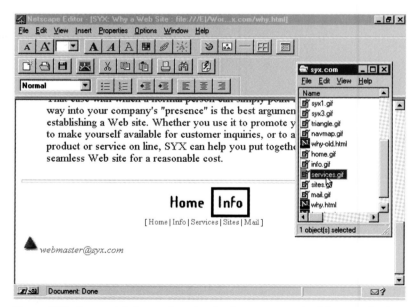

Figure 12.2 For straightforward navigation image maps, the fakery method works just fine

Frames: The High-Tech Look

Frames were introduced by Netscape. If you've ever worked with a spreadsheet program that allowed the screen to be broken up into panes, or if you've ever split the screen of a word processor, then you already have an inkling of what frames look like and do on Web pages. Frames are subdivided regions of the screen. Each frame can behave more or less as a separate Web document, so it's not just a fancy type of table! Frames can also contain links that point into other frames, such that clicking in one frame (a navigation area across one side of the screen) can result in a change in another frame (perhaps in the large, primary area). Figure 12.3 shows a Web consultant's site that uses frames in its high-end, "full service" area.

The problems with frames can range from the minor to the more severe. Truth be told, not all browsers recognize them (frames have a built-in way of offering substitute pages to browsers that don't "do" frames). Compounding this is the nuisance that the standards are still in flux, with Netscape and Microsoft, typically, tossing around changes.

You've seen frames in action already if you've used Netscape's Page Wizard (see Chapter 4). That design uses three frames for instructions, input, and preview.

Figure 12.3 The PINT (Powell Internet Consulting) Full Service page features a two-frame design

And finally, there are the more fundamental issues of whether they're worth the bother, or just plain ugly (not to mention wasteful of precious screen real-estate!).

Surely, in the long run, some method for keeping fixed navigation tools, or other features on the screen, while allowing other sections to change will be widely adopted. And frames might just be the way to do it, but that's not yet perfectly clear.

The ultimate problem with frames is that the coding can be quite tricky, depending on what behavior you want, and poorly coded frame pages can cause unreadable pages that may even crash a user's browser! So with that in mind, we'll give you a quick overview of the essential frame tags and then leave it up to you to decide whether you're too busy to tackle the project yourself.

Pages with frames actually consist of several different Web documents: a main document containing the frame coding and the alternative coding (for non-frame users); and additional documents, one for each frame. Create the documents that will be shown in the frames first, using the techniques you've learned throughout this book. Needless to say, if the frames will be used to display contents from a variety of pages, you'll need to create a document for each page that might be shown in that frame.

The master document for such a page, instead of the usual <BODY> and </BODY> tags surrounding its contents, has the <FRAMESET> and </FRAMESET> tags.

The FRAMESET tag can have either a ROWS or a COLS tag inside, specifying the number of rows or columns, and the relative sizes of each. (If you want rows *and* columns, you have to start with one—rows, for example—and then nest additional FRAMESET tags inside the first one to add columns.) The size of a row or column can be expressed as an absolute number of pixels, a percentage of the screen width or height, or as a variable (indicated by an asterisk) equivalent to a share of the unassigned space.

Inside the FRAMESET tags, you can include nested FRAMESET tags or FRAME tags. Within the FRAME tag itself, you can nest a number of other tags, of which the following are the most important:

habits & strategies

You're best off just typing the codes up yourself because Netscape Editor (as of version 3.0) will not be any help with making frames.

habits & strategies

To make a link that can eradicate all the frames and return the browser to full-screen mode, you can add the tag TARGET="_top" to the link. (There has to be an underscore character before the word top.)

- SRC="*URL of source document for frame*"
- NAME="*named target anchor*" (optional)
- SCROLLING="YES, NO, *or* AUTO" (AUTO means the frame will be able to scroll only if it needs to (i.e., if the contents don't fit)
- NORESIZE (to make the frame boundary immovable)

To supply substitute content for browsers which are not frames-sensitive, you can enclose normal HTML markup (created ahead of time in Netscape Editor, if you like) between the <NOFRAMES> and </NOFRAMES> tags and inside the FRAMESET tags.

To make a hyperlink bring up a page in specific frame, add the attribute TARGET="*named target anchor*" to the standard <A HREF="*URL*"> tag.

The most basic type of Web page using frames is one that contains a navigation frame that doesn't change and a display frame that changes depending on which link is clicked in the navigation frame, such as the one shown in Figure 12.4.

Figure 12.5 shows a more complicated frame layout designed by

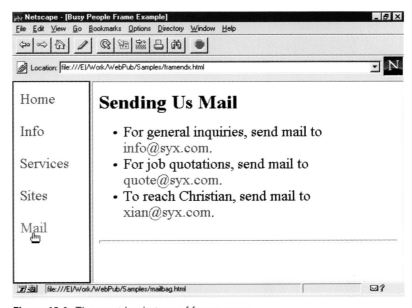

Figure 12.4 The most basic type of frame page

Always ask yourself "Who's going to manage and update this site?" before proceeding.

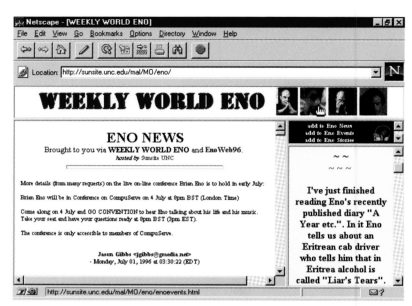

Figure 12.5 Enough frames for you at **http://sunsite.unc.edu/mal/MO/eno/**?

Malcolm. My technical editor tells me he's seen a page with eight frames! Hard to imagine how they would all fit.

DYNAMIC PAGES

There are two senses in which pages can be dynamic. In the more basic sense, pages that cause the server to *do* something (besides serve up another page) are dynamic. At the high-end, pages that are created on-the-fly by database or other software, are also said to be dynamic. The rest of this chapter will discuss the slightly more run-of-the-mill tricks to make your pages responsive: forms, simple CGI scripts, and JavaScript.

Get 'em to Fill Out Forms

It's one thing to learn the coding that makes forms look good on the screen. Although it's a little tedious, it's not too hard, and if you've become accustomed to working with dialog boxes, then you'll recognize the different types of doodads that make up a form. However, it's another thing entirely to get the forms working on the "back end" (the

habits & strategies

If you want a form, you'll have to enter the tags by hand, since Netscape Editor (as of version 3.0) doesn't know from forms. Microsoft Internet Assistant for Word for Windows does have a form tools built in, which you can access by selecting Insert | Form Field. (You can download Internet Assistant from **http://www.microsoft.com.)**

Forms also look different in different browsers. To see for yourself, find a form page and look at it first in Netscape and then in Lynx (the text-only UNIX browser).

server side) so that when your reader fills out a form, something actually happens. Finally, it's yet another matter to actually entice any of your visitors to fill out the form. The last part is an issue for the marketers and the psychologists. We'll show you, briskly, how to construct forms in this section.

An alternative to mail forms (which require CGI scripts) is the mailto: URL. This can be combined with options to force specific headers to conform to a preset format. For instance, to enable readers to send mail to one of the authors of this book, we could insert the following into a Web document: <A HREF="mailto:xian@syx.com?Subject=WebPublishing">Send mail to Christian about the <CITE>Web Publishing</CITE> book</A>.

But what can you do with forms? Any time you want to solicit input from a reader and then respond to what's typed, a form is the way to go. Popular uses include order forms (for online commerce), search forms (for searching the site or the entire Net), and mail forms (for directing feedback into a database or archive).

Constructing a Form in a Document

Forms begin with <FORM> and end with </FORM>. The FORM tag includes two additional attributes: METHOD= which can be set to GET or POST (it depends on the server—use GET if you're not sure); and ACTION="*URL of script for form*".

Just before the end of the form, it's customary to include two buttons: one for submitting the filled out form, and one for clearing the form and starting over. The tags for each, respectively, are <INPUT TYPE="submit" VALUE="*optional text, instead of 'Submit'*"> and <INPUT TYPE="reset" VALUE="*optional text, instead of 'Reset'*">.

In the middle go the tags for the form itself—that is, the various blanks and choices that make up the form. The tags for form-entry include the following:

- <TEXTAREA NAME="*name*" ROWS=x COLS=y>*optional suggested default text* </TEXTAREA> for text boxes;
- <INPUT NAME="*name*" TYPE="*text, password, checkbox, radio, int, hidden, submit, reset*" VALUE="*default value, if any*" SIZE="*optional size*" MAXLENGTH="*optional maximum length*"> for the various input types available.

243

Some people use form codes as funky design elements without actually trying to send form data to a server (e.g. inserting a drop-down list for amusement or using a Submit button just to function as a link to another page). This misuse of the tags generally does no harm.

(Note: passwords appear as asterisks when entered; multiple checkboxes can be checked at once; include the tag CHECKED to have a checkbox checked by default; only one radio button can be selected at a time; int stands for integer, whole number; hidden is used for information that gets sent with the form no matter what);

- <SELECT NAME="*name*" SIZE="*optional number of items to be shown at a time*"> and </SELECT> for drop-down lists (described next).

The SELECT tag produces a drop-down list. To create items for the list, include them between the SELECT tags, starting each one with <OPTION>. To assign a default option to a list, use <OPTION SELECTED> for that one instead. Add MULTIPLE to the SELECT tag to allow more than one item from the list to be selected at once.

Figure 12.6 shows a form utilizing many of the input options.

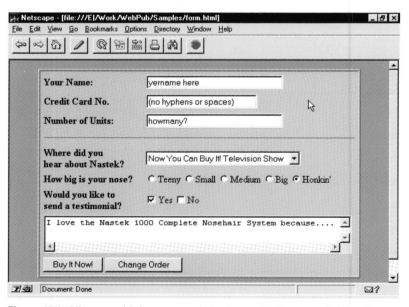

Figure 12.6 Like we said, forms are relatively easy to draw up. Getting them to do anything is another matter

To make your form do anything, you'll need to write or borrow a script and put it, or have it put, on your server (see Chapter 13 for more about servers). We'll touch on scripting in the next section. Still, while the *functionality* of your form may be in the hands of a programmer, the appearance, layout, order, and structure of your form is a design issue that you should consider as carefully as you would the rest of your home page.

trends

It's a good bet that Netscape Editor will eventually come with an image map creator, a frame editor, and a forms tool, if not by version 4.0, then soon thereafter.

habits & strategies

*You can also just download or copy a full-featured version of the MetaCrawler form from **http://www.metacrawler.com/ form.txt**. Edit out any of the options you don't want to offer on your page.*

Connecting to an Existing Back End

One type of form you can create that will work without requiring you to set up the back-end code is a simple search form hooked up to one of the public search engines or directories. You can offer a visitor to your page a direct line to one of these browser resources with the willing cooperation of the search-engine people, who appreciate the hits.

One of our current favorite search sites is the MetaCrawler, which submits links to a wide range of indexes and directories and then returns its results in a consistent format. To add direct form access to the MetaCrawler engine, just insert the following code into your document:

```
<CENTER>
<TABLE BORDER=1 CELLPADDING=12>
<TR><TD><FORM METHOD=GET ACTION="http://www.metacrawler.com/cgi-bin/nph-metaquery.p">
<H3 ALIGN=CENTER>Search 'em All with MetaCrawler:</H3>
<input name="general" size=36>
<input type="submit" name="searchType" value="Find!">
</FORM></TD></TR></TABLE>
</CENTER>
```

The simple search-engine front-end form should look like this on your page:

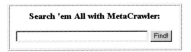

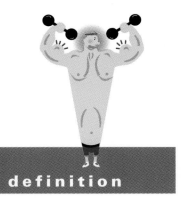

CGI: Common Gateway Interface, a standard set of commands for passing information back and forth between a Web server application and the computer it's running on, including other software running on the same computer or network.

Writing, Stealing, or Hiring Scripts

Both traditional server-side image maps and forms require the cooperation of a server to function properly. The ingredient that tells the server what to do, how to do it, and when is the CGI script.

If you've ever worked with macros within a program such as WordPerfect or Word, then you have some idea of what a script does. You may also know that the devil is in the details, and understanding what to do in principle is a far cry from writing up a script with no bugs in it, putting it in the right place on a server, and getting it to work.

The most common type of CGI script is the type that responds to submitted form data. The script file, containing the actual text instructions is the file referred to in the ACTION="*URL*" part of the <FORM> tag (discussed in the previous section).

definition

script: A small-scale program consisting of instructions designed to respond to varying circumstances with different actions and results.

For a query form that's connected to a database, for example, when the user clicks the Submit button, the following things happen:

1. The browser sends the request entered into the form to the server, which starts the specified script.
2. The script carries the request to the database manager program (this is why it's called a *gateway* script, because it negotiates between the server and other functions of the host computer or network) and submits a query in a format the database understands.
3. The database returns a result to the script and the script then formats it into an HTML document, which it passes back to the server.
4. The server sends the newly created Web document to the browser, which displays it as the next page the reader sees.

A good script will also contain provisions for errors, and other variations on the purpose of the form.

Scripts can actually be written in any language that the server computer understands. They can even be, although rarely are, full-fledged, compiled programs.

Another common type of script is the sort that negotiates between a simple form and a mail server, enabling people to send replies in a consistent format. Another is the type that keeps track of how many visitors have come to a page —"You are visitor number XXXX since our hit-count script last broke down!" A more sophisticated type of script, coupled with a regularly updated index of a site, can enable your readers to search your site by entering key words into a simple form.

Clearly, a thorough discussion of CGI scripting could fill a whole book (and has already filled many). For the most common uses of scripts on the most popular servers (see Chapter 13 for more on servers), you can probably find an existing script that works. More than likely though, you'll have to adapt it slightly to the particular configuration details of your server and the machine it runs on (that's the rub).

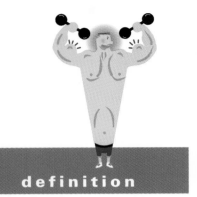

definition

JavaScript: Formerly LiveScript, a set of programming instructions that can be inserted into a Web document and interpreted by a browser to produce interactive or variable effects.

bookmark

For archives of existing scripts, try Matt's Script Archive (http://worldwidemart.com/scripts/).
For more on CGI scripting, try Introduction to CGI Programming http://www.usi.utah.edu/bin/cgi-programming/counter.pl/cgi-programming/index.html), the CGI Book—Links (http://www.cgibook.com/links.html), or Mike's Guru Page (http://www.cs.unc.edu/wwwc/public/capps/guru.html).

Netscape Editor permits you to insert JavaScript code, but it doesn't understand it or interpret it.

Dabbling with JavaScript

The final way to jazz up Web documents—one that's within reach of a normal busy person—is to incorporate JavaScript commands into your Web document. JavaScript is not the same thing as Java itself. Nor is it the same thing as the CGI scripts described in the previous section. Java is a much more fully functional programming language. CGI scripts run on the server side. JavaScript is interpreted by the browser (on the client side).

As with CGI scripting, it's not really possible to learn the ins and outs of JavaScript casually. However, there are a number of useful existing JavaScript routines that you can borrow and adapt for your own pages, the same way you might borrow and adapt someone else's HTML code.

Examples of popular, simple JavaScript routines include a scrolling, possibly annoying to some, "marquee" message in the browser's status bar, and a script using a command called "onMouse Over" that puts explanatory text instead of the destination URL in the status bar when the user positions the mouse pointer over a link.

bookmark

More JavaScript information can be found online at the JavaScript Index
(***http://www.c2.org/~andreww/javascript/***), *the Unofficial JavaScript*
*Resource Center (****http://www.intercom.net/user/mecha/java.html****), or*
*Netscape's own JavaScript page (****http://home.netscape.com/comprod/***
products/navigator/version_2.0/script/script_info/index.html)http://
www.infohiway.com/faster/index.html).
An organization that calls itself the Bandwith Conservation Society
(***http://www.infohiway.com/faster/index.html***) *has a nice archive of*
*cut-and-paste JavaScript examples (****http://www.infohiway.com/***
javascript/).
You can also search for specific types of JavaScript applets at
http://altavista.digital.com *by entering* **applet:keyword,** *such as*
applet:spreadsheet.

WHAT'S NEXT?

If you've made it this far, then it's time to stage your site and start
testing it. If all seems to work well, then you're ready to publish the site
and start promoting it. The last chapter of the book will tell you how to
find or hire a server for your site, how to publish your documents there,
and what to do next.

Publishing and Promoting Your Web Site

251

FAST FORWARD

CHOOSE A SERVER FOR YOUR SITE ➤ *pp. 254-258*

1. Decide which platform your server will run on.
2. Choose a server product (try the Serverwatch site at **http://www.serverwatch.com** for the latest information).

HIRE A SERVICE PROVIDER
TO HOST YOUR SITE ➤ *pp. 258-259*

1. Visit The List (**http://www.thelist.com**) to scout for likely providers.
2. Ask potential providers some of the following questions:
   - Can I make updates to the site directly myself or will I have to send changes to a Webmaster and wait for them to be posted?
   - How much traffic does the server handle now? What are the quotas (included in the base charge) for disk storage space and server traffic?
   - Will I be permitted to run CGI scripts from your server?
   - What provisions, if any, are there for password protection, commercial transactions, or other forms of privacy or security?

PUBLISH A WEB DOCUMENT ➤ *pp. 260-262*

1. Click the Publish button.
2. Click in box marked Upload files to this location and enter the FTP address to which you can send your files.
3. Press TAB, type the username, press TAB again, and type the password.
4. Check Save password if you want to avoid typing it again in the future.
5. Click OK.

PROMOTE YOUR WEB SITE ➤ *pp. 263-267*

- Submit announcements to major search engines and directories.
- Announce your site on mailing lists and Usenet.
- Offer to trade links with related sites.

As we discussed near the beginning of this book, there's a difference between *authoring* pages and *publishing* them. Most of this book has dealt with the ins and outs of creating your own pages and linking them together into a coherent Web site. Eventually, there comes a time to put the site you've been developing out onto the Net, in public, or onto your organization's intranet, in private. Either way, when you've built your pages and tested them and everything looks fine (or at least "good enough for now"), then you have to transfer or send your pages to the server where they'll be made available to Web browsers.

If you've been working on a public site for a potentially wide audience (of customers, perhaps), then you'll also have to devote some time to announcing and promoting the site, so it doesn't get lost in the vast shuffle of the Web. (We'll also explain exactly how to "push" your pages out onto a public site, using Netscape Editor.)

Whether you run a Web server yourself or hire out that work, you'll have to consider what type of security is offered by the server software, both in terms of keeping internal company matters private and for providing commercial security, so that you can provide safe transactions to your customers. You'll also have to think about whether your organization needs its own domain name.

As for promoting the site, sure, it's easy to visit all the major index and directory sites and submit the address of your new site, but going beyond that level requires an ability to find the appropriate interest groups and announce your site to them without spamming. You'll need to keep an eye out for opportunities to promote the site in the real world (off the Internet) as well.

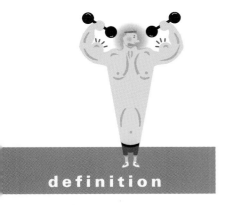

definition

Spam: *To indiscriminately send unsolicited (especially commercial) e-mail to a huge, unsuspecting audience.*

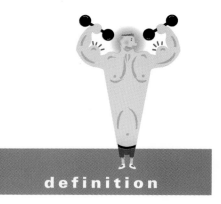

Web farm: A large Internet Web server site that hosts many smaller Web sites.

FINDING A SERVER

There are two ways to publish your Web site on an Internet server. One is to set up and run your own server on a machine connected to the Net. The other is to pay a provider to host your site for you on an existing server. Depending on the size of your organization and your budget, either solution may work for you.

If you "rent" space on a provider's server (or "Web farm"), you settle for less security and control of your site. It may be difficult or cumbersome to update your site and you may not be able to install the software you want there (such as a RealAudio server). On the other hand, the site will probably be faster to access and cheaper to maintain. Cost issues are subtle and have to be weighed against the bandwidth you're getting.

Maintaining your own site can be expensive when you take into account all the labor, equipment, lines, servers, and so on. You also won't be able to have the fastest type of connection (a T3). On the positive side, you can integrate your Web presence with your other Internet servers, such as e-mail, and you'll have total control over the site.

Interestingly, both small firms and firms with huge sites often prefer Web farms. Large Web sites (think Disney) have to farm out their surplus resources to offset costs whereas small sites can't afford their own links. Most entities in between prefer to maintain their own site.

Running Your Own Server

Running your own server can mean setting up a 386 PC clone running the free Linux operating system and free UNIX Web-server software, such as Apache or httpd, over a round-the-clock ISDN link. It could also mean being given access to a directory on a server already set up for your organization, or setting up and maintaining a network with a fast, dedicated gateway to the Internet on a high-end P6 workstation running Windows NT and Netscape, Microsoft, or other Web-server software.

No matter what solution you choose, and you should solicit as much advice as possible for your specific circumstances, you must be

*If you choose one of the more
popular servers, then it's more
likely that you'll be able to find
working examples of useful
scripts. With up-and-coming
servers, you may have to do
more script development
yourself.*

*It is also possible to install the
freeware Linux operating system
(a UNIX clone) on PCs, from the
386 up to the Pentium, and then
run one of these UNIX Web
servers on a PC.*

prepared to maintain a 24-7 Internet presence if you intend to run your
own server. Decide what sort of computer you are going to run your
server on. Do you have a spare PC? Ideally, you wouldn't want to share
your server machine with other processor-intensive tasks, such as
database management.

The type of server software you choose depends primarily on
what sort of computer you plan to run it on. We'll tell you about the
most popular servers on the most common platforms. More importantly, we'll tell you how to keep up-to-date as these facts change. New
developments emerge on the Net all the time, so you'd do well to know
how to keep abreast of the news.

Other considerations that will help you decide among servers are
cost (some are free, some are cheap, some are expensive), available
support, whether the server is "commercial" (can handle transactions,
whether you need this capability now or in the future), and the speed
or efficiency (throughput) of the server.

Servers for Windows

Most Windows Web servers are designed to run on the 32-bit versions
of Windows (NT and Windows 95), although a few do run on the earlier
16-bit versions (Windows 3.11 and Windows for Workgroups). Windows is a bit of a latecomer to the server game, but Windows NT already
threatens to become a dominant platform. Netscape's two servers are
the most popular, but Microsoft is aggressively pushing the Internet
Information Server as the best solution for integrating the back end of
a Web server with Microsoft Office software. O'Reilly's WebSite is also
a bit of a sleeper, with positive critical reviews (see Table 13.1).

UNIX Servers

At one time, all the sites (or nearly all) on the Web were UNIX sites.
Many of the large service providers still rely heavily on UNIX machines
and most scripts and other add-ins for Web sites are still developed on
the UNIX side first, before being ported to the Macintosh and Windows
platforms.

The first Web server was CERN's httpd. This was succeeded by
NCSA httpd, which is still in circulation. An update of the NCSA server,

Vendor	Product Name	Price	Download Site	Remarks
Microsoft (**www.microsoft.com**)	Internet Information Server (**http://www.microsoft .com/InfoServ/**)	Free	**http://www.microsoft.com/ infoserv/iisinfo.htm**	part of NT Server, no remote admin, some security
Netscape (**home.netscape.com**)	FastTrack,formerly Communications Server (**http://www.netscape. com/comprod/server_c entral/product/ fast_track/**)	$295	**http://cgi.netscape.com/ cgi-bin/123server.cgi** (60-day eval)	most popular, not secure for commerce
	Enterprise Server, formerly Commerce Server (**http://www.netscape. com/comprod/server_c entral/product/ enterprise/**)	$995	**http://home.netscape.com/ comprod/mirror/server_ download.html** (60-day eval)	most popular, secure for commerce
O'Reilly & Associates (**www.ora.com**)	WebSite	$249	**http://software.ora.com/ download/** (eval)	fast, easy, sophisticated
	WebSite Pro	$499	**http://software.ora.com/ download/** (eval)	commercial (security)

Table 13.1 Windows Web Servers

called Apache, is currently the most popular UNIX-based solution (see Table 13.2).

Macintosh Servers

While the makers of other Web server software always promise that a Macintosh version is on the way—*real soon now*—it seems that for the time being, the field of Mac servers is not crowded. Your choice is essentially between StarNine's WebStar, the free MacHTTP product from which WebStar evolved, and a new integrated server product (it does FTP and gopher too) called InterServer Publisher (see Table 13.3).

Vendor	Product Name	Price	Download Site	Remarks
Apache Group (**http://www. apache.org**)	Apache	Free	**http://www.apache.org/ dist/**	Based on NCSA httpd, most popular server
NCSA (**http://hoohoo.ncsa. uiuc.edu**)	httpd		**http://hoohoo.ncsa.uiuc.edu/ docs/setup/Download.html** or **http://hoohoo.ncsa.uiuc.edu/ docs/setup/OneStep.html**	no official support
Netscape (**home.netscape.com**)	FastTrack, formerly Communications Server (**http://www.netscape. com/comprod/server_c entral/product/ fast_track/**)	$295	**http://cgi.netscape.com/ cgi-bin/123server.cgi** (60-day eval)	not secure for commerce
	Enterprise Server, formerly Commerce Server (**http://www.netscape. com/comprod/server_c entral/product/ enterprise/**)	$995	**http://home.netscape.com/ comprod/mirror/server_ download.html** (60-day eval)	most popular, secure for commerce

Table 13.2 UNIX Web Servers

Vendor	Product Name	Price	Download Site	Remarks
InterCon (**http://www.intercon. com**)	InterServer Publisher	not set	**http://www.intercon.com/ products/interserverp.html**	
StarNine (**http://www.starnine. com**)	WebStar	$499	**ftp://ftp.starnine.com/pub/ evals/webstar/ webstar.sea.hqx**	(formerly MacHTTP), the most popular Macintosh server
	MacHTTP	$65 (educational) $95 (others)	**http://www.starnine.com/ machttp/machttpsoft.html** (30-day eval)	predecessor to WebStar

Table 13.3 Macintosh Web Servers

habits & strategies

Keeping Up with the Latest Server News

We know the information shown in the preceding tables because we haunt certain Web sites that function as centralized clearinghouses for Web server facts and news. By far the best single site is Serverwatch (**http://www.serverwatch.com/**). Yahoo has good information as well, as do others such as clnet (there's also a good list of links at Serverwatch), from time to time.

bookmark

*Serverwatch is at **http://www.serverwatch.com/**. Yahoo's server page is **http://www.yahoo.com/Computers_and_Internet/Internet/World_Wide_Web/HTTP/Servers/** and there's a subpage just for Macintosh. Another site that compares servers is **http://www.proper.com/**.*

Finding a Host for Your Site

The alternative to maintaining your own server is to hire out the hosting, and a good deal of the day-to-day maintenance of the site (also known as the Webmastery), to a service provider.

It may be possible or preferable to get your Web site hosted by your e-mail or Internet access provider, but it's not necessary. You don't even have to limit yourself to providers with local access phone numbers. As long as you have some sort of Internet access already, you can negotiate a separate hosting arrangement with any provider on the Net.

Service providers can also offer "domain name service" to give a domain name for your company (www.yournamehere.com), either for a separate fee or as part of a company-account package. See "Establishing Your Internet Presence" (the next section) for more on domain names.

When negotiating with a potential host for your site, here are some issues to consider and questions to ask them:

- Can I make updates to the site directly myself or will I have to send changes to a Webmaster and wait for them to be posted?

- What type of machine houses the site and what Web server software runs on that machine (see the previous section for more on server software)?
- How much traffic does the server handle now? What are the quotas (included in the base charge) for disk storage space and server traffic?
- Will I be permitted to run CGI scripts from your server?
- Is there an existing library of common scripts already available at the server?
- Are there any supplementary servers or facilities available for building a Web presence (such as mailing list software, hypernews or other discussion group tools, and so on)?
- What provisions, if any, are there for password protection, commercial transactions, or other forms of privacy or security?
- How dependable is the server? What provisions are in place for backing up the server in case of failure?

Establishing Your Internet Presence

Beyond setting up a Web site, to establish a full-fledged Internet presence, you'll probably want to establish your own domain name (that is, if you or your organization has not already done so). Primarily, this has cosmetic advantages. A short URL focused on your company name is more memorable and "attractive" than a longer one where your company name hangs off the end of your provider's address.

As with servers, you can either register and maintain your own domain name or you can have your provider do it for you. To maintain your own domain, you'll need access to at least two computers on the Internet that are running name-service software (this is why it's often easier for providers or other centralized entities to do this, rather than individuals), and you'll need to fill out the appropriate paperwork for InterNIC (**http://www.internic.net**) and pay $100 for two years of service.

Most providers offer domain name service as part of a package (particularly for business accounts) or as a separate billable service. This can mean the difference between a nice short URL like http://www.yourcompany.com, or something along the lines of

habits & strategies

Perhaps the best advantage of having your own domain name is that it's completely "portable." You can change your host provider or move a site to different machines and keep the address exactly the same.

http://www.providername.com/yourcompany/ or, worse yet, http://www.providername.com/~yourcompany/. Then again, some providers offer a quick and dirty method in which your home page URL is not at the "root" of a server but in a subdirectory, something like http://www.yourcompany.com/yourcompany. This is not as good, since anyone entering just the www. . .com part will actually end up at your provider's home page instead of yours. It may cost extra for the "site redirection" option (which gives you your own "root" address), but it's worth it.

TRANSFERRING FILES AND POSTING PAGES

Whether you maintain your own server or contract for someone else to host you, you will have to deal with sending (also called publishing or uploading) your Web documents and related media files to the server. Traditionally, this was done using either FTP (File Transfer Protocol), to transfer the files, or Telnet (remote login), to log in directly to the remote site and create the file there. You can still do it this way, but you don't need to since Netscape Editor can be set up to publish your files for you automatically.

"One-Button" Publishing

When the time comes to publish a document to your server, start by clicking the Publish button.

This will bring up the Publish Files dialog box (see Figure 13.1). The first time you do this, the Publishing location area of the dialog box will be blank, but in the future, it will remember your previous entries and you'll be able to reuse them if you want to.

- If you just want to publish the current document, you can ignore the upper half of the dialog box.

- If there are any graphic images in the file, the Images in document radio button will be selected, and all graphics will be sent. To prevent sending a graphic, click Select None, and then re-select only the graphics you *do* want to send.
- If you want to include additional documents, graphics, or other files in this single upload, click the All files in document's folder radio button, and then select the specific files you want.

In the Publishing location area of the dialog box, click in the Upload files to this location box and enter the FTP or HTTP address to which you can send your files. Quite often, a location on the Net has both an HTTP address for public viewing and a parallel FTP address for sending files. You may have to check with your system administrator or service provider to get the proper address. FTP addresses start with ftp:// and usually include more directory information than the corresponding HTTP address. For example, to place a file called path.html at the address http://ezone.org/ez/e8/path.html, you'd have to send it to ftp://ezone.org/./public_html/ez/e8/.

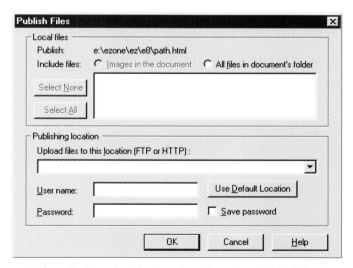

Figure 13.1 Specify the publishing location of your file in this dialog box

CAUTION

If you tell Netscape Editor to save your password, then anyone using your computer will be able to publish files to your Web server, so be careful.

On many UNIX Web servers, your page still won't be visible until you set its mode to "world readable." To do this, you'll either have to telnet to your site, and then issue the command chmod o+r filename, or ask your system administrator to do so for you.

(The single dot indicates the "home" directory that you're logging into. Many UNIX Web servers are set up so that user's Web pages are located in a subdirectory called public_html.)

After entering the URL to publish to, press TAB and then type the username for the account associated with the Web server (that may be a personal account, a corporate account, or a special Webmaster account). Press TAB again and type the password. Check Save password if you want to avoid typing it again in the future. Then click OK. Netscape will switch to a browser window to make the connection and will then send the file. If you've made an error in the address, username, or password, Netscape will tell you that you made an error. Click OK and try again.

If everything is in order, Netscape will send the file or files to the server and inform you that it's doing so.

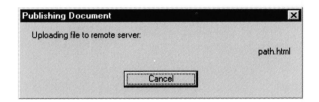

It's called one-button publishing because there's this handy Publish button on the toolbar, but it's always at least two buttons! Next time you need to send a page to the same location, you can click the Publish button and then just click OK to publish the document (see, two buttons!).

Your Default Publish Location

It's also possible to browse to your server using its FTP address and then just drag files from the folder windows directly onto the Navigator screen. First, though, you have to set up a default publish location. To do so, select Options I Editor Preferences and select the Publish tab of the Editor Preferences dialog box (see Figure 13.2).

Enter the address you publish to in the Publish to box. Enter the public URL of the site in the Browse to box. And then enter the username and password information for the publish-to address (as you did in the previous section).

*Once you've set up a default
publish location you can click
the Use Default Location button
in the Publish Files dialog box to
select it in the future.*

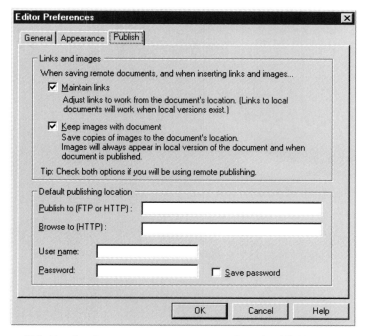

Figure 13.2 Here's where you can enter your preferred publishing location

Any time you want to jump directly to the site you've been publishing to, select Go | Default Publish Location in the Netscape browser window.

Another way to publish a document is to browse to the upload location and then drag a document directly from a folder to the Netscape window (see Figure 13.3).

PROMOTING YOUR WEB SITE

Once you get past the wonder of it all—the fact that you can set up a tidy little Web site just "down the road" from CNN, the White House, and Sony—you realize the catch: how will anyone ever find you? The Internet and the Web get more complicated and crowded every day. There's no "space" to run out of, but you still have to work to make sure that people who might be interested in your site can find it. So publishing is one thing, but findability is the key.

CAUTION

You can't publish a file by dragging it if you've got a document on the screen in Netscape. You have to be viewing an FTP directory to do this. Also, sending text files by this method will sometimes create problems with line-ending characters (when going from some computer platforms to others).

To prevent robots from adding some of your pages to their indexes, see http://info.webcrawler.com/mak/projects/robots/norobots.html.

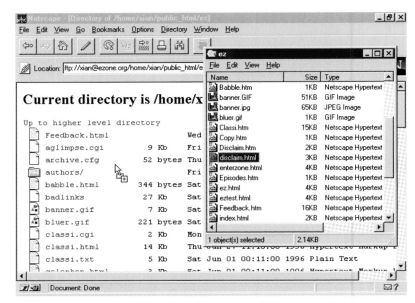

Figure 13.3 Publishing a document by dragging directly to an FTP site in the Netscape browser window

There are really two ways to publicize your site online. The first is to submit the URL of your site to every directory and search engine you can find (excluding perhaps the uncategorized "What's New" pages out there). Easy, but tedious. The second way is more subtle and is more in line with the traditional meaning of the word "networking." To make a site visible from the many avenues on the Internet, you have to communicate with other people who publish on the Net or participate in discussion groups. You have to tell them, by e-mail or in public posts, about your site and trade hyperlinks with sites that have common themes or interests.

Submitting Announcements

All directory and search engine sites send robotic indexing programs around to browse the Web, follow links, and add sites to their databases. But why wait until they find you when you can go directly to the source?

The first step is to write an announcement describing your site, what makes it unique, and its intended audience. If your announcement

h a b i t s &
s t r a t e g i e s

Don't underestimate the
importance of promoting your
site in the "real world." Be sure
to put your URL on business
cards and letterhead and
advertising or marketing
campaigns to promote your
site's address.

is long (more than a few paragraphs), create a companion, condensed version of it, since many of the sites allow only short statements. (Many of them won't even use your text, for that matter.)

After that, you just repeat the following process as many times as you can stand:

1. Browse to a search, directory, or "what's new" site (see Table 13.4).
2. Choose the Submit URL or equivalent option.
3. Enter your site's Web address and as much of your announcement as the form permits.
4. Submit the information.
5. Check back after a week (or whatever lead time the site recommends) to make sure that your site is now listed.

Table 13.4 lists the major sites to which you should consider submitting your URL. New search sites appear all the time, so visit some of the centralized search sites such as Netscape's Internet Search page (**http:// home.netscape.com/home/internet-search.html**) or clnet's Search.com (**http://www.search.com**) and scan the sites, adding any new ones to your list.

Site Name	URL
100 Hot Web Sites	**http://www.100hot.com**
AltaVista	**http://altavista.digital.com**
Excite	**http://www.excite.com**
G.O.D.	**http://www.god.co.uk**
HotBot	**http://www.hotbot.com**
InfoSeek Guide	**http://guide.infoseek.com/**
Internet Resource Meta-Index	**http://www.ncsa.uiuc.edu/SDG/Software/Mosaic/ MetaIndex.html**
Lycos	**http://www.lycos.com**
Magellan	**http://www.magellan.com**
OpenText	**http://www.opentext.com/omw/f-omw.html**
Point	**http://www.pointcom.com**

Table 13.4 Sites for submitting your URL

Site Name	URL
Submit It!	**http://www.submit-it.com**
W3 Web Servers	**http://www.w3.org/pub/DataSources/WWW/Servers.html**
WebCrawler	**http://www.webcrawler.com**
Whole Internet Catalog	**http://gnn.com/gnn/wic/**
WWW Virtual Library	**http://www.w3.org/hypertext/DataSources/bySubject/Overview.html**
Yahoo	**http://www.yahoo.com**

Table 13.4 Sites for submitting your URL. *(continued)*

Your first stop should be Submit It! (**http://www.submit-it.com**), since that page contains links to most of the other relevant sites. Submit It! is a sort of mega-form that you can use to submit to multiple search and directory places. It's not quite as easy as it sounds since you still have to submit to each individual site, one after another, but at least many of them are all in one place (see Figure 13.4).

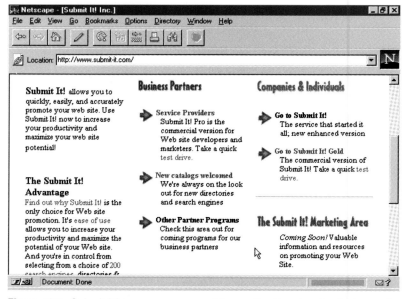

Figure 13.4 Submit It! saves you some of the surfing time involved when submitting your site's address to multiple places

Networking and Trading Links

To really have a "presence" on the Net, you have to spend time communicating with people one-to-one via e-mail and one-to-many via discussion groups. Going beyond just responding to e-mail from visitors to your site, this means you're also putting the URL of your site in your e-mail signature so that anyone who gets mail from you gets at least a minimal, classified ad-type plug for the site. Here's Christian's signature to give you an idea:

```
- -
Christian Crumlish                    http://www.pobox.com/~xian
Internet Systems Experts (SYX)            http://www.syx.com
Enterzone                               http://ezone.org/ez
```

Also, you have to be on the lookout for organizations and groups of people on the Net and from other Web sites, that deal with topics similar or related to your own. For a business site, this may mean tracking down other vendors, suppliers, and so on, whose products and services relate to your own. As long as they're not your competitors, there's no reason why they shouldn't want to trade links with you.

What do we mean by trading links? Most sites have at least one page somewhere with links to related sites. If both your site and the site of the person you're trying to coordinate with have such a page, offer to list their site on your page in return for a reciprocal link on their page. The same way any big city can be thought of as myriad smaller villages, all overlapping and to some extent interconnected, so can the Web be thought of as a conglomeration of many such smaller webs of interrelated sites. You want to find or create that sort of smaller web to which your site should belong and make sure that you're well linked into it.

As for Usenet newsgroups and mailing lists that deal with subjects related to the topic of your site, feel free to send announcements to them when your site is first published and whenever you make major changes or updates to it.

MAINTAINING AND UPDATING A SITE

Even after you've finished creating the site, published it to the Net, *and* worked day and night promoting it, your job is not necessarily done! There's a distinction here to be made between designing (and building) a site and "Webmastery." Every site needs a Webmaster in the same sense that every mail server needs a postmaster. Someone has to fix things that go wrong, respond to basic e-mail, keep the server running, and—perhaps most importantly—post updates and changes to the site as they evolve.

The questions you must ask are, "Who will do this job? Me? My service provider? An assistant?" If you hire Web designers to create or enhance your site, don't assume that they will also take over the Webmaster chores unless it's written into the agreement.

If it falls to you to oversee a site, you may want to invest in a site-management program such as Adobe PageMill (on the Macintosh side) or Microsoft Front Page (on the Windows side). These programs, at the very least, make it easier to keep all your internal links up to date if and when you make changes to the overall structure of the site.

bookmark

*Serverwatch maintains an up-to-date list of site development and management tools (**http://www.serverwatch.com/sdm.htm**). Yahoo also has a good section on this subject (**http://www.yahoo.com/ Computers_and_Internet/Internet/World_Wide_Web/HTTP/Servers/ Log_Analysis_Tools/**).*

Webmastery also involves analyzing the access logs that most servers generate. If you pay a service provider to host your site, ask them if they can give you your access stats on a regular basis. (They may just point you to a page at the site that can generate reports for you.)

A Web site will wither away if you don't revisit it often to improve its appearance, content, and organization, or to add up-to-date information to it. To avoid chaos, you need to establish a clear, simple system for making updates. Only one person should have the final say in what gets posted, and all changes should be made in some safe staging area and tested before being posted to the public site.

THE END

Well, that's all folks. By now you know more than enough to design, build, and publish a site. You have the tools at your fingertips to develop the Web site of your dreams, and soon, if you put your ideas to work, the world will beat a path to your home page.

Index

Y